A Practical
Guide to
Graduate Research

To David

A Practical Guide to Graduate Research

Molly Stock
Professor of Forest Resources
University of Idaho

McGraw-Hill Book Company

New York St. Louis San Francisco Auckland Bogotá Hamburg
Johannesburg London Madrid Mexico Montreal New Delhi
Panama Paris São Paulo Singapore Sydney Tokyo Toronto

This book was set in Times Roman by Black Dot, Inc. (ECU).
The editor was Stephen Zlotnick;
The production supervisor was Diane Renda.
The cover was designed by Victor Bastante.
Project supervision was done by The Total Book.
The Book Press, Inc., was printer and binder.

A PRACTICAL GUIDE TO GRADUATE RESEARCH

5 6 7 8 9 0 BKPBKP 9 8 7 6 5 4 3 2 1

ISBN 0-07-061583-7

Library of Congress Cataloging in Publication Data

Stock, Molly.
    A practical guide to graduate research.

    Bibliography: p.
    Includes index.
    1. Research—Methodology.   2. Universities and
colleges—Graduate work.   I. Title.
Q180.55.M4S86   1985   001.4   84-7927
ISBN 0-07-061583-7

Contents

Preface

Students learning to do research are regularly faced with discrepancies between the rational model of the research process provided by texts and teachers and the realities of how research is actually conducted. This book explains some of these discrepancies, and is intended to complement and augment the help provided by a research advisor on a research project. Specific tasks and sequences of activities guide the student through the graduate program and through the development, execution, and completion of the research project. Topics range from planning the program to publishing the first research paper and emphasize subjects of special concern and importance to graduate students. Practical criteria are provided to help the student make informed decisions at many critical stages in their program—choosing an advisor and a project, evaluating progress and performance, and developing realistic expectations of his or her own progress, advisors, and the graduate program itself. Techniques are described for facilitating open communication and for reducing anxiety and discouragement.

The book is written to be used both independently by graduate students and their faculty advisors (especially those in the natural or physical sciences) and as a text for graduate-level research methods courses. While specifically aimed at thesis-oriented students, major portions of the book can be helpful to students in nonthesis options as well.

For initiating the chain of events that led to this book, I am grateful to William Beveridge, whose book, *The Art of Scientific Investigation*, gave me my first inkling of what research really involves. Many colleagues and friends shared ideas and provided encouragement during all stages of development of this book. I especially thank Noland VanDemark and Joe Novak at Cornell, Allan Wicker at Claremont Graduate School, Bob Coulson at Texas A&M, Gerald Lanier at SUNY-Syracuse, Kareen Sturgeon at Linfield College, Jack Kimbrell, Robert Lentz, Michael Shook, June Lipe, and Ross Miller at Washington State University, and Gary Machlis, Sam Ham, Ali Moslemi, Ron Force, and Mark LaMoreaux at the University of Idaho. For providing materials to help illustrate this book I thank Jo Ellen Force, Kevin Williams, Cinda Cone, Greg Kallio, and Kipp Kilpatrick. Above all, I am grateful for the patience, intelligence, and industriousness of the many graduate students with whom I have worked during the past several years. Their enthusiasm to learn about research, their obvious need for the sorts of practical information presented here, and their candid comments and criticisms were the catalyst for the writing of this book. As an observer and facilitator in their struggles to master the research process and to overcome the many obstacles inherent in graduate study, I continue to learn as much as they.

Molly Stock

Chapter 1

The Research Process

During my doctoral research program, I ran across a book that discussed the role of intuition and chance in research.[2]* I vividly recall the fascination with which I read this book, and especially the mixed feelings of enlightenment and relief as I discovered that much of what I had been doing—the "mistakes," the changes in direction and perspective—were legitimate and, in fact, necessary stages in learning the research process. In working with graduate students since then, I have found that most of them, including many who are well along in their research, are similarly confused about what research really entails. The performance criteria that they learned to excel at as undergraduates—studying for grades in a structured setting—no longer pertain in any important way, but the criteria for the new task—research—are ill-defined.

---

*Numbers throughout refer to end-of-book references.

Obviously, much fundamental and potentially very helpful information is not available to graduate students when they need it most. Lacking this information, graduate students struggling through their first research projects often feel that much of what they are doing is wrong because it does not match the models provided by traditional definitions of research and by published research papers which they believe establish the new performance standards. Without research experience, the discrepancies between these models—between what the students think they should be doing and what researchers actually do—can be disorienting and discouraging.

What *is* research? Is it testing hypotheses? Gathering data? Why does our society make learning to do research an integral part of most graduate degree programs? Why would anyone want to spend 2 to 4 years of his or her life learning how to do research? Why would anyone be motivated to spend 18-hour days on a research project, as most graduate students do, and enjoy it? The answer to these questions is simple: research is discovery, and discovery is an exciting adventure. The 1 percent inspiration that provides the discovery makes the other 99 percent of the endeavor that is tedious and frustrating worth the effort.

Before discussing practical aspects of research—what doing research really entails and how it relates to your research program —we must start by briefly reviewing the theoretical framework upon which research is based. Nearly everything you do in graduate school relates back to development of a full understanding of this approach and of an ability to use it effectively, creatively, and productively.

Research, the systematic search for new knowledge, usually begins by discovery of existing knowledge, by seeking information from various traditional and authoritative sources of such knowledge: professors, books, journals, and the like. At the same time, we continually synthesize this information and add to it as we have ideas that tie together the things we have learned, as we begin to gain real understanding and to see gaps in this knowledge. Traditionally, research then adds another step to the discovery process, a gathering of evidence, a testing stage—to falsify or to validate that which seems correct. Research incorporating a testing stage is considered *scientific research,* regardless of whether the tests involve controlled laboratory experiments or collection of information from naturally occurring phenomena (through survey results or field observations). While the other methods of learning are useful and important in research, they have fundamental limitations that make this testing stage necessary. For example, tradition, authority, and "common sense" once led to the erroneous belief that the earth is flat. It was only when people began to test this notion by studying the stars or sailing off over the horizon that knowledge was advanced and the correctness of the idea could be judged. Scientific research can thus be viewed as an extension of tradition, authority, and intuition (the generation of ideas). Science tests ideas generated by intuition in some objective, public, and repeatable way that may reveal their incorrectness. Thus although there are several ways that we personally can attain knowledge, only two—intuition and science—can provide us with truly new knowledge. Intuition and science are the key components of research.

SCIENTIFIC RESEARCH

Scientific research has been formally defined as *the systematic, controlled, empirical, and critical investigation of hypothetical propositions about the presumed relations among natural phenomena.*[15] Simply stated, this means that scientific research is the *testing* (systematic, controlled, empirical, and critical investigation) *of ideas* (hypothetical propositions about the presumed relations among natural phenomena) generated by intuition. Scientific research involves a way in which we generate ideas and a way in which we treat ideas once they are generated.

Some corollaries arise from these definitions. First, ideas that are not testable in some objective way (such as concepts of "goodness") are not within the realm of science or scientific research. Second, any idea that has not yet been tested but that is testable, whether it comes from tradition (the literature, for example), authority (our advisors), or intuition, can become the focus of a scientific research project. Third, testing is only a part of research.

The *scientific method,* the basis for scientific research, consists of several steps:

Observation
Problem definition
Hypothesis
Test
Theory

First, observations are made of some natural event. Next, pertinent questions are asked and the specific problem to be addressed is defined. Then a hypothesis is generated. A *hypothesis* is simply an educated guess about the relationship between two or more phenomena (that is, what you think is happening). The fourth step in the scientific method is the testing stage. This step is what makes science and scientific research unique, but by itself it does not, as is sometimes believed, constitute science or research. Based on test results, the hypothesis is rejected, accepted, or, in most cases, modified.

If a hypothesis is found to be true in a wide variety of situations, a theory—a general explanation—is developed. The basic aim of science is to make and to use theories, to find general explanations for natural events. In this way, we obtain understanding, prediction, and control of natural phenomena.

Much scientific research, however, is not obviously theory-oriented but rather is aimed at the shorter-range goal of understanding a particular relationship between events. Regardless of how limited or small-scale your own research is, it should always be viewed as a building block for theory and its breadth of application should be carefully considered. More simply, you are obligated, at the end of your research project and in writing your thesis, to consider broader applications of what you have discovered.

The rational model of the *research process* follows the scientific method closely:

Observation: familiarization, literature review, coursework, and practical experience (building background)

Problem definition: specific questions asked
Hypothesis generation: objectives defined and appropriate
methods selected for testing hypothesis
Testing: data collected, analyzed, and interpreted
Hypothesis accepted, rejected, or modified

First, a general problem area (a research topic) is defined and
pertinent observations are made. The researcher becomes familiar
with the problem in many ways—reading, thinking, discussing,
exploratory field or laboratory work, and (for the graduate
student) coursework. From this observation phase, a more specific
area needing further study (that is, needing clarification or understanding) is identified and the specific problem to be addressed in
the research is defined. During these first stages in the project, the
researcher struggles to formulate the problem in his or her own
mind and to ask the basic questions properly, based on current
knowledge in the area.

On the basis of the questions asked, the hypothesis or
hypotheses are constructed and their implications are deduced.
That is, the researcher makes a specific guess (hypothesis) about
what is going on and then determines if the hypothesis, as stated,
leads to a clear-cut test or experiment. If not, the hypothesis is
reformulated so that it is testable. At this stage, the original
problem and hypotheses may be changed (broadened or nar-
rowed) or even abandoned.

A common misconception of beginning researchers is that the
research itself does not begin until the project has been designed
and a structured acquisition of numerical data has begun. Research starts long before this phase, with reading, thinking, and
exploratory experiments or tests. The formal data-gathering phase
of the research is only a part of the research process and is
certainly not, in most research, the most important part. What
happens before and after formal testing is often much more
critical.

Finally, the relationship expressed by the hypothesis is tested
by observation and possibly experimentation. Then, on the basis
of the test results (the research evidence), the hypothesis is
rejected or accepted and this information is fed back to the

original problem, which then may be altered or reformulated as dictated by the evidence. This last step, from test results back to hypotheses and theories, makes the rational model of research both cyclical and sequential.

This is the way good scientific research is done and the way it is formally described in the literature. As a theoretical framework for understanding research, this description (the rational model) is

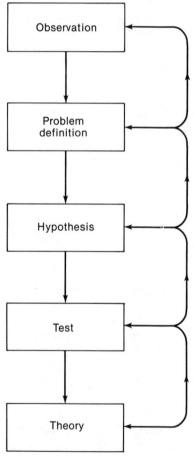

FIGURE 1-1 The research process.

tidy and satisfying. However, as a practical guide to initiating and carrying out your first research project, it is not very helpful. For beginning researchers, it can create an oversimplified and misleading expectation of what research involves. It should be viewed only as an idealized guide. A concept of research drawn from the scientific literature is no more likely to fit the actual enterprise than is an image of a culture drawn from a tourist brochure or a language text.[17]

Actually doing research on a day-to-day basis is very different from this idealized outline. Research is a much more chaotic and dynamic process than the outline implies. For example, in reality, research consists of a number of closely related activities that overlap continuously rather than follow a strictly prescribed sequence. Rarely, if ever, is one step completed before the next is begun. Journal articles suggest that research has been carried out in the idealized step-by-step sequence. This linear style of writing is certainly justified for the sake of clarity and economy in presenting research findings, but it must not be mistaken for the way that research is actually done.

In addition, there is usually no clear end point to a research project. Limits must be set on a project for convenience and communication. These limits—end points—are imposed on a process that is essentially endless. Furthermore, researchers commonly select specific research problems for nontheoretical reasons and only afterward search the literature to seek a justification for making a particular problem the subject of their investigation.

Research also involves many additional activities that are rarely, if ever, mentioned in publications or reports. These include many logistic activities related to research management—for example, making decisions about the kinds of data needed and the most efficient way of collecting them, developing and pretesting equipment, planning a budget and obtaining funds, and allocating and training personnel. Research also involves a number of intellectual processes related to the generation of ideas. Last, the essential act of communicating research through talking and writing is not a simple, automatic outcome of the research process. Effective communication about research involves further knowledge and skills.

Chapter 2

The Graduate Program

The graduate research project must first be discussed in the context of the graduate program as a whole. Regardless of where you decide to go to graduate school, this program has purposes and constraints that directly affect the way you will approach, carry out, and complete your first research project.

The graduate program usually consists of a mixture of courses related to your chosen specialty, and a research project. Some of the courses may be more difficult than those you took as an undergraduate, but they are all an extension of a mode of learning with which you are familiar and probably quite successful: a structured format with scheduled class periods, exercises, tests, and grades. The structure of the research project will be less familiar to you. While you will continue to learn things new to you in your coursework, the research project will teach you to be a discoverer in the true sense, to develop ideas and information that extend beyond what is currently known and that cannot be taught in the classroom. The aim of the graduate program is thus much more than acquisition of knowledge. While you will learn more about the specific area you have chosen to study, the program will also teach you principles of independent problem solving that have broad application. These principles will have value regardless of whether you are eventually employed in the specific field that you now choose to study (and it is very likely that you will not). Because this approach to learning is probably new to you, the criteria for setting your expectations and evaluating your performance will seem much less clear than those for coursework. This apparent lack of definition can lead to some problems that are fairly predictable but largely avoidable.

If you arrive at graduate school near the beginning of a semester, perhaps the most pressing concern will be to get registered for a few appropriate courses. Before doing this, you must get advice from someone, such as the graduate student advisor for your college or your department chairperson, who is familiar with the curriculum and the graduate school requirements and can help you choose courses to get you going in generally the right direction. Other graduate students and faculty in your interest area may also help. Once you have registered and are taking some classes, you are in somewhat familiar territory and can begin planning your graduate program in earnest.

SELECTING AN ADVISOR

One of the first steps in working out a satisfactory graduate program is selecting a thesis advisor. The advisor is usually a professor whose research is in your area of interest, and who can help you develop a graduate program and a research project in this area. You are not expected to have chosen an advisor before you arrive at graduate school, although some students do. If you seem to have a choice among a number of faculty specialists in your area of interest at your chosen institution, you may want to take some time to gather information about these people so that you can make a more informed choice. Because no one person is ideal for the role of advisor, and because your first choice may not be able to take on another student, selecting an advisor may take some

---

Things to check out when you arrive at graduate school*

Minimum credit hour requirements for the degree in various categories (lower division, upper division, thesis)?

Graduate school requirements (advisors, committees, qualifying exams, etc.; forms to fill out and sequence of events)?

Assistantships and financial aid, leave, payroll, and tax information?

Work opportunities (irregular help, work-study, etc.)?

Office space and key policies?

Library location, service, and hours?

Computer facilities?

Typewriters and word-processing facilities?

Availability of secretarial services?

Phones?

Use of college/university vehicles?

Graphics services, artwork, photography?

Use of laboratories, shops, greenhouses, etc.?

Job placement services?

---

*Ask faculty members, secretaries, the graduate advisor, the main graduate office personnel, and read any graduate student handbooks for your college or university.

FIGURE 2-1

effort. Talk to the various faculty members and graduate students in the area to obtain pertinent information.

Sternberg[27] suggests that the bottom line for an advisor is that he or she be there for the length of one's project; a warm body present is better than any absent warm body. (The only thing worse than an absent advisor, Sternberg suggests, is an advisor who is present but hostile.) Does the professor have tenure (permanent employment status)? Is he or she planning a sabbatical leave in the near future? Is he or she near retirement?

Other criteria for selecting an advisor are that the person be at least moderately interested in your work, be accessible, be respected professionally by other faculty and students, read papers within a reasonable time after their submission—and read them critically, offering ample comments and suggestions—and be rigorous about methodology and project design.

You might also seriously consider a professor's actual research record. If you are seeking some sort of model or mentor to emulate, you will want to pick a good one. Regardless of the national ranking of the particular school, quality and quantity of research performed by individual faculty members vary considerably. Although nearly all professors have a stated research specialty, not all are actively doing research in this area and not all are equally knowledgeable and up to date. Whether because of interests or assignments, some may be dedicated primarily to teaching, others to administration. While these duties are certainly necessary and worthwhile, they may hinder such individuals from giving you personal attention and guidance for your research.

In your discussions with potential faculty advisors, look for signs of recent research productivity—mainly grants and publications. Publication has gotten some bad press as being the major criterion, above teaching, upon which university professors are judged. Nevertheless, regular publication in refereed (that is, critically reviewed) journals and books is a good sign that a professor is active in his or her field. (A publication record that consists largely of articles in meeting proceedings, abstracts, reports to agencies, or papers published by the home institution itself is a cause for some suspicion about the quality of a professor's research.) You might also consider the number and types of conferences and meetings attended by a professor and the types of talks given (were they *research* talks?).

In all your discussions, however, keep an open mind. As with certain popular social activities, people who talk a great deal about the number of publications on which they are working often have a mediocre research record. And you may also find, as you talk to the professors in your area, that one is much more compatible with you than the others, for reasons quite unrelated to any objective criteria.

As you talk to other graduate students—some working with the particular professor and some not—be aware that advice from students, although candid, is often based on hearsay rather than actual knowledge. As with faculty, research competence can vary a great deal among graduate students, and a student's ability, as well as personality factors, may influence his or her view of a particular professor. And although professors may point out individuals who are good advisors and competent researchers, they are rarely candid about who is *not* a good advisor or researcher.

An important consideration may be whether you should choose to work with someone established and well known in a particular area or with a less well known, relatively new professor. You should be aware, if you are not already, of the ranking system for university professors. New professors (Ph.D.s fresh from graduate school) are usually hired as *assistant* professors. After an evaluation period of several years, they may be promoted to *associate* professor and be given tenure. Those associate professors who contribute much to their institution and to their profession, nationally and internationally, are eventually promoted to the rank of *full professor,* or, simply, professor. Thus a professor's rank—assistant, associate, or full—tells you something about his or her experience.

In spite of obvious differences in experience, you may get a lot more personal, detailed attention to the development and progress of your research project from a new faculty member working to establish himself or herself in a research area. On the other hand, a senior professor with a good record often has a more finely honed sense of judgment about projects and directions and can give you more rigorous and incisive advice and criticism as you progress. A well-known researcher can often generate funds to support your work more easily, and may therefore provide you with a greater chance to attend professional meetings, hire temporary help, and buy supplies and equipment. However, by choosing an advisor who is well known, you risk being seriously neglected, as the best people are often much busier and in greater demand than those either new to the business or not as good. These trade-offs must all be considered. You can't have it all. It used to be especially wise to seek out a well-known person who could, at the end of your program, help get you a job through his or her contacts and good reputation. Today, this old-boy network is less effective for this purpose than it used to be, as affirmative action has opened jobs for competition among all qualified persons. Nevertheless, letters of recommendation from established and respected scientists are still an important part of getting your foot into the employment door.

Through all this, try not to worry excessively about selecting an advisor. A good advisor can be a big help to you, but the quality of the advisor is not the critical factor for the success of the program—you are.

The Advisor's Role

Early in your program, discuss with your advisor his or her general philosophy about research projects and his or her expectations of you. But what should *you* expect of your advisor during your graduate program? Only rarely do you find a student who is completely happy with the amount and type of feedback and support provided by the advisor. Resentment, frustration, and disappointment are common. Why is this so? Are that many advisors really neglecting their advisees and not directing them properly? Although this may sometimes be the case, I believe that most problems arise from unrealistic expectations.

Having a competent researcher as an advisor does not always make the learning of research easier. Because many researchers learned their craft almost entirely by trial and error, some believe that their students should too. They were thrown in the water and learned to swim, so they believe (to some extent perhaps correctly) that this is a good way to sort out the qualified from the unqualified researchers of the future. More commonly, faculty researchers are genuinely too busy to take the time they would like to work with each student. In addition, memories of the anxieties, questions, and self-doubts that experienced researchers felt about their own early research efforts tend to fade as they gain self-confidence. And even when there is a real attempt at communicating about research and the graduate program, the critical, conscious, methodological processes are usually emphasized over the equally important creative processes. A realistic perspective of what other people should or can do for you during your graduate program can make your work much more satisfying and your interactions with your advisors more positive and productive.

Most graduate students tend to judge their advisors by the same criteria they applied to their undergraduate teachers. They expect to be supervised closely when they must learn to supervise themselves, however painful it may be at first. The research project is supposed to be an independent effort. For this reason, the advisor's involvement with your program and your project will probably be much less than you expect at the outset. On the other hand, you are expected to come to the advisor when you need help. This doesn't ensure that you will get the advice you seek, but the probability is certainly greater than if you don't take this initiative. Similarly, it is up to you to keep your advisor current on your progress. Later on, if your advisor has not been closely involved with your study, invite him or her to visit your study site or laboratory setup.

For many reasons, having an advisor who is overly helpful, friendly, or supportive—whether because he or she is a new and eager assistant professor or an established research scientist with a vested interest in a particular project—is not always desirable. Research, being a discovery process, requires that a certain number of mistakes be made. You will learn more by making some mistakes and from pursuing some half-baked ideas than if your advisor assumes a major role in the development of your project. You are learning to be an independent thinker, not a second-rate technician. By directing you too closely, an advisor can actually reduce the chance that you will turn up something genuinely new and that you will learn to synthesize information from your own background, interests, and experience. Without the challenge of struggling with your problem, you may not develop the necessary level of mastery and confidence in doing research. You may finish with a quality thesis, but you may also leave with the feeling that you couldn't have done it on your own. And perhaps you couldn't.

By now, most of you have heard of the value of a mentor to guide your career. Ideally, a mentor will sharpen your professional and political skills, instill confidence, help clarify goals, and lend a hand up the ladder. You may envision the advisor-advisee relationship as a mentor-protégé arrangement, but this is rare. Even if you are lucky enough to have an excellent mentor during your graduate career, be aware that the connection between mentor and protégé is, by definition, temporary, and that the true measure of the relationship's success is the protégé's growing ability to function alone.[26] From the start, the bond is meant to be severed.

Don't seek to be what your advisor is, or to learn only what he or she knows, but to develop your own channels of thought and activity so that the probability of discovery is maximized. Judge your advisor by how well he or she helps you do this, by how much you are encouraged to follow your own ideas and how often you are challenged to reexamine your beliefs.

Attitudes, Conflict, and Compatibility

There is no such thing as *the* researcher. Researchers are people of very dissimilar temperaments, doing different things in very different ways. Douglas McGregor developed some management theories that can be helpful in working with your advisor and others on your research project.[20] McGregor said that most people's attitudes toward work are based on one of two underlying sets of assumptions. He called them Theory X and Theory Y. Theory X people believe that the average person dislikes work and will avoid it if possible, that most people must be controlled, directed, or threatened with punishment to get them to work well, and that the average person prefers to be directed, wishes to avoid responsibility, and has relatively little ambition. As leaders, such people are authoritarian and very conscious of their position, have little trust in their subordinates, and feel that pay is a just reward for work, the only reward that will motivate the worker. They give orders and demand that they be carried out. No questions are allowed and no explanations are given. Theory X group members assume little or no responsibility for their performance and will merely do what they are told. Productivity is usually high when the leader is present, but drops in his or her absence.

In contrast, Theory Y people believe that the average person likes work and responsibility, that people will exercise self-direction and self-control in achieving their objectives, that they will not only accept but seek responsibility, and that the intellectual potential of the average person is only partly utilized. Theory Y leads to a democratic leader and a group in which decision making is shared. Criticism and praise are objectively given, new ideas and changes are welcomed, and a feeling of responsibility is developed. When the leader is forced to make a decision, the reasoning is explained to the group. Quality and productivity of work are generally high regardless of whether the leader is present.

These attitudes can help explain successful advisor-advisee relationships as well as many of the conflicts that occur between research advisors and graduate students. Thinking about your own attitudes toward work and supervision can help you understand the perspectives of others. The ideal situation is when both student and advisor have similar attitudes toward work. Conflicts can arise when the advisor and advisee are of basically opposite types. A Theory Y professor will become frustrated by the apparent lack of motivation shown by a Theory X student. The student will be disappointed with the professor for not providing clear rules and guidelines. In contrast, a Theory Y student who has a Theory X advisor will feel restricted and patronized. These attitudes cannot be changed easily but they can be recognized for what they are. If necessary, you should either change advisors or learn to live temporarily under a different set of rules.

Another potential source of conflict lies in your approach to research, and your advisor's. Some people are innately more speculative, more creative and imaginative in their work than others are. Such people tend not to pay much attention to detail. Others tend to be more systematic, believing that progress is to be made by careful accumulation of data. Graduate research is perhaps easiest for the more systematic type of individual because virtually all data collection is done by the student. And such a student will work well with either a similarly systematic advisor or even with a speculative advisor who is full of ideas but vague about methodology.

An advisor who is concerned with details and approaches research in a more methodical way will probably have problems working with a more creative and speculative student. However, the training that the creative student gets will complement his or her talents in important ways. He or she will be forced to focus attention on the critical and methodological processes in research and will gain an understanding of a side of research that he or she may never actually do alone again. With a similarly speculative and creative advisor, the nonsystematic student will get little direction in methodology. These are, of course, rather broad generalizations, and many notably successful advisor-student relationships are exceptions to them.

TIME SCALE

In developing your graduate program—determining both the courses you will take and the duration and type of your research project—you must first consider when you expect to finish. This deadline may be modified as you progress, but some estimate of the project's duration must be made at the outset. A master's program, with thesis, generally ranges anywhere from 18 months to 3 years, with 2 years being about average at most institutions. In some departments and with certain advisors, an 18-month program is most common. A Ph.D. program generally ranges from about 2 to 4 years, if a master's degree is obtained first.

It may be possible to go straight for a Ph.D., omitting the master's thesis project entirely. For several reasons, such a straight-through Ph.D. program is generally not recommended. The master's program gives the student a chance to learn the research process, skills that can be refined and developed later on in a more complex and demanding Ph.D. project. Much more independence and professionalism, as well as a more substantial contribution to one's field, is expected in a Ph.D. program.[7] Because most beginning graduate students really don't have a clear idea of what research entails (although many think they do), it is usually best to begin work on a master's project, which is more limited in scope. Once that is completed, you will have a much better idea of what is involved in doing research and can initiate a Ph.D. project with greater mastery and self-confidence.

APPOINTMENT OF THE GRADUATE COMMITTEE

Your advisor and others—students and faculty—can help you determine what people, representing various specialty areas, might appropriately serve on your graduate advisory committee. Including your advisor, a graduate committee usually consists of a minimum of three people for a master's program, or four people for a Ph.D. program. One of these people is usually chosen from an outside or related specialty area.

Once you have the names of some potential committee members, talk to them about your program. Tell them why you are in graduate school and what you would like to do. Ask them about their work. Get an idea of how helpful they might be to you during your graduate program. If you think they would be appropriate, ask them if they will serve on your committee. Because serving on a graduate committee generally entails much less time than serving as a major advisor, it is usually fairly easy to persuade a person to serve on your committee.

Selecting a committee does not in any way limit the number of people from whom you can solicit help and advice during your graduate program. As you develop a wider range of contacts, many other people may prove exceedingly helpful to you, and you should not hesitate to ask for their advice. For one reason or another, however, it sometimes becomes appropriate to change the formal structure of your committee—to replace a member or even switch to another major advisor. Because of the enormous potential for generating hard feelings in such cases, great care should be taken to make such a change with tact and courtesy.

Working with Your Committee

In working with your graduate committee, remember that it is *your* graduate program, that it is *your* responsibility to ensure that it goes well. You must be actively involved in all stages of its planning, evaluation, and completion.

During your first or second semester, you will develop a study plan outlining the courses you will take to fulfill the institution's requirements. Once you have begun to prepare the study plan, with your advisor's help, you will need to meet with your committee to discuss it and agree on it as a group before you finalize it for submission to the graduate school. Because you will want to demonstrate your seriousness and commitment to graduate school, and to establish a businesslike working relationship with your committee, considerable preparation should go into this meeting. First, you must arrange the time and place. Find a time convenient for all members of the committee, then reserve a room for the meeting through the main departmental or college office.

Next, prepare written handouts to provide the committee members with information to help them give you the best possible advice at the meeting. If this material is given to them either before or at the beginning of the meeting, and includes pertinent information presented clearly, concisely, and systematically, the committee members will be in a much better position to use their experience to guide you in the right direction at this early point in your program. With proper preparation, the objectives of a committee meeting can usually be accomplished in an hour or less.

Here is what you should prepare:

1 A page or two summarizing your *background* as shown in Figure 2-2. Copies of your transcripts are not adequate. At the top of the first page, list degree(s), major(s), and universities. Then list the relevant courses you have taken, grouped under appropriate headings (such as forestry, math, statistics, genetics). Don't list every course you have ever taken. Make some intelligent decisions about what to include and exclude. If any other information is relevant, such as certain work experience, provide this information too, in summary form.

2 A statement of your *goals,* to be presented either orally or as a written handout—what you would like to study, what you want to become, anything that will help your committee members know what they need to know to advise you best. Have a tentative research topic defined. Don't worry if this information repeats what you may have told each person in individual discussions earlier. It is important that all information be fresh in everyone's mind for discussion.

3 A list of your *proposed coursework* for the entire graduate program (by semester with dates and courses listed by title, abbreviation, and number as shown in Figure 2-3). When you aren't sure, list alternative courses for discussion or simply put in a question mark. At the bottom of the page, summarize credits by category: undergraduate, graduate, research, and total credits.

All written material provided to your committee should be neatly typed, as should all work that you do during graduate school. Inability to type is no excuse. Pay someone to type for you,

```
[NAME]
[UNIVERSITY], B.S. 1985


                        Previous Coursework

    Mathematics                                          Credits

        MS 12          Analytical Geometry and Calculus     4
        MS 150         Math Models for Life Sciences        3


    Physical Sciences

        PS 11/12       General Physics                      8

        CH 10          General Chemistry                    8
        BC 21          Organic Chemistry                    4
        BC 122         Biochemistry                         4


    Biological Sciences

        BIO 13         Plant Biology                        4
        BOT 164        Taxonomy of Vascular Plants          4

        ZO 14          Animal Biology                       4
        ZO 153         Invertebrate Biology                 4
        MB 127         General Microbiology                 5
        ZO 158         Parasitology                         4

        ZO 156         Animal Ecology                       4

        GN 162         Principles of Genetics               3


    Entomology

        ENT 26         Introductory Entomology              4
        ENT 140        Taxonomy of Elementary Orders        4
        ENT 153        Taxonomy of Advanced Orders          4
        ENT 143        Forest Insect Ecology                3
        ENT 149        Economic Entomology                  3
        ENT 261        Entomology Seminar                   2
```

FIGURE 2-2 Background summary for committee meeting.

take a typing course, or learn to use a computer word-processing facility.

At the beginning of the meeting, after you have introduced members who may not know each other, distribute handouts and

```
[NAME]

                        PROPOSED COURSEWORK

For M.S. degree in Forest Resources to be completed May 1986:

    Fall 1984                                              Credits

    FOR 527       Forest Genetics                             4
    FOR 465       Forest Protection                           3
  ? FOR 507 ⎫ one   Integrated Pest Management                3
  . FOR 524 ⎭ of ?  Advanced Silviculture                     3
              these                                          ──
                                                            10

    Spring 1985

    FOR 528       Forest Tree Improvement                     3
    FOR 494       Models for Resource Decisions               4
    ENT 468       Forest and Shade Tree Entomology            3
    GEN 535       Ecological Genetics                          3
                                                            ──
                                                            13

    Summer 1985

    FOR 500       Thesis                                      4

    Fall 1985

  ? FOR 569 ⎫ one of   Advanced Forest Entomology             3
  . ENT 541 ⎭ these    Advanced Insect Ecology                3
             ?
    FOR 352       Forest Pathology                            4
    FOR 500       Thesis                                      4
                                                            ──
                                                            11

    Spring 1986

    FOR 501       Seminar                                     1
    GEN 522       Statistical Genetics                        3
    FOR 500       Thesis                                       8
                                                            ──
                                                            12

    ----------------------------------------

    SUMMARY:   500-level (not research)      20
               400-level                     10
               300-level                      4
               Thesis research               16
                                             ──
                             TOTAL           50
```

FIGURE 2-3   Proposed study plan for committee meeting.

tell your committee what you want from them. Be straightforward and honest as your program is discussed, and listen carefully to suggestions for alternative courses or instructors. Occasionally, one or another committee member will see no need for some aspect of your program that you strongly wish to include. At one meeting I attended, a physiologist and an ecologist disagreed about the proposed research project. One perceived it as an excellent laboratory study. The other thought that the laboratory work was extraneous and that the research should involve only the student's planned field study. Needless to say, these viewpoints influenced the committee members' suggestions for the proposed graduate program. Although occurrences such as these might be unsettling, they will not present any great problem if you remember that it is your program and the ultimate decision about what you do is yours, provided that your advisory committee can come to an agreement.

As you develop your study plan, think of it as a contract with the graduate school. That is, even though you may plan to take several courses beyond the minimum requirements of the particular graduate school, it is usually best to submit, on paper, only the minimum list of courses acceptable to your committee, with the agreement that you will audit or take for credit certain other courses as time permits. This will maximize the probability of your completing your program on schedule. The entire plan should not hinge upon everything going in an optimal way for the specified time period. Consider how you might be able to fulfill requirements for the degree even if you broke your leg just before the field season, or had to take two months off in the middle of the semester because of a death in the family. Build this flexibility into your study plan by *not* including all that you think you might be able to do while you are feeling ambitious and are not yet immersed in, and preoccupied by, your research.

A major goal of the graduate program is to teach you the value and joys of independent learning, to send you beyond the classroom to exploration and discovery on your own. One sign of progress in attaining these goals is a change in attitude toward classwork. New graduate students usually arrive eager to continue building their stores of knowledge through coursework. They enthusiastically scrutinize the catalog and compile long lists of courses to take, often many more than the minimum required by the graduate school. As students become more involved in research, however, and find out how much more satisfying (often, in fact, addicting) learning through research can be, interest in coursework typically wanes considerably. If the graduate program is successful—from the point of view of both the institution and the student—the student will find himself or herself more and more anxious to finish classwork and get back to the laboratory, the field, or the computer terminal. A type of mental maturation occurs, a switch from an interest in accumulating existing knowledge to an interest in original, independent thinking.

The very least you can do, in developing your course schedule and study plan, is to try to schedule the smallest possible number of courses during your last one or two semesters. Even after the study plan has been submitted to the graduate school, however, it can be changed with fairly little effort as long as your committee agrees to the change, and the minimum requirements of the graduate school are fulfilled.

Call other committee meetings and meet individually with members several times during the course of your graduate program. Appropriate times would be when you are finalizing your research plan and at intervals during the research itself. Meet at times when the committee's advice can have an impact. Don't, for example, decide to meet the day after you've finished gathering data. A more beneficial time would be just before you begin to collect it, at a time when your committee can review your plan, suggest improvements, and detect deficiencies before it is too late. Summarize what you have accomplished and how you propose to proceed. An agenda for the meeting is not inappropriate. Written progress reports at various stages, even if they are only a page or two long, are extremely helpful to all concerned.

While you will want to meet with your committee to show progress or discuss plans, it is also very important to meet when things are *not* going well. Often a meeting called when you are feeling discouraged and overworked can be very reassuring and can get you back on track. The main desire of your committee members is to help you, not to evaluate you. If you need help, ask for it. The committee serves no useful function if all they do is see you when things are going well or at times when their advice can

have no influence on your program. Don't let feelings of incompe-
tence or inadequacy inhibit you from aggressively seeking help,
advice, and the learning you came to graduate school to get.

"Dumb" Questions

Many students come to graduate school with the erroneous but all
too common notion that they are supposed to be very smart. And,
like most people, they know they are not as smart as they would
like to be, so they feel that they should at least *act* smart, because
most of the other students really are. It may reassure you to know
that 99 percent of the rest of the graduate students are worried
about the same thing. You are, indeed, expected to be smart, but
not to be particularly knowledgeable. Stop worrying about asking
"dumb" questions. No one expects you to know everything. I have
seen communication and mutual support break down entirely
among groups of graduate students preoccupied with appearing
intelligent to their fellow students and faculty. Make a great effort
never to pretend to know more than you know. Ask questions.
Ask *lots* of questions. Don't hesitate to admit that you don't know
and seek further information. Life will be much easier for you and
the quality of your graduate program will be enhanced. You will
worry less, learn more, and communicate better. If you listen to a
seminar or read a paper while worrying in the back of your mind
that you are not smart enough to understand it, a great deal of
needless anxiety is generated and the learning process is short-
circuited. If you don't understand something that you think might
be of value if you knew it, be the first to say so.

　　If you adopt this practice, when you are put in a position of
not knowing an answer or of being shown that what you did was in
error, you will not feel overly distressed. You will simply and
unapologetically admit you don't know or that you hadn't known
any other way to do something at the time, and, without embarrassment, you will seek further information. This ability will be of
considerable comfort in initial dealings with your committee, in
oral examinations, and in giving seminars or talks about your
research.

　　In asking questions, a useful technique is *paraphrasing.* You
can get others to clarify their remarks by asking, "What do you

mean?" or "Please tell me more." If you are still unsure of the answer, repeat how *you* understood it and allow the other person to respond. In essence, you are checking to make sure you understood the point correctly, just as you do when someone tells you a phone number. If you repeat it incorrectly, the speaker will correct you. Use this technique frequently to let other people know what their statements or ideas mean to you. Whenever possible, put information in your own words and give the speaker a chance to correct it. "It seems to me that you're saying . . ." or "Are you saying that . . .?" The other person may say that is indeed what was intended, or that it wasn't, or that it was only part of it. Paraphrasing thus increases the accuracy of communication and of how much you learn. It also conveys your interest in what the other has to say. Bad listening is faking attention to the speaker. We have all developed methods to appear to be listening while we enjoy the privacy of our own thoughts without intrusion by the speaker. It is perhaps not overly cynical to estimate that an average of half the people in any audience are not really listening. Good listening is not relaxed or passive. It is hard work. To paraphrase, you must become an active listener and pay close attention to what is being said.

PLANNING

The key to successfully completing graduate school is not brilliance or even inspiration, but rather, organization and persistence. During this early stage of your graduate career, begin planning your program, based on the time period you have allotted for it. Start by listing all that you must do within that time frame if you wish to obtain a graduate degree. Put these items in chronological sequence, as best you can. To do this, collect general and graduate university catalogs and outline the steps leading toward fulfillment of the degree requirements. If necessary, talk to your advisor or to someone in the graduate school office to get help in developing this outline. Many graduate schools already have a standard form available for helping you keep track of your progress. Many of the steps involve filling out and submitting to the graduate school, in a particular sequence, various forms that demonstrate your completion of various stages in your program and your progress toward the degree.

Then begin to rough out your overall timetable, including the main stages of your research project, even if the project is only vaguely defined. A good way to do this is with a bar chart as seen in Figure 2-4. Start filling out this chart by adding a bold vertical line at your estimated time of completion and then decide how you will go about finishing everything by this deadline.

With a reasonable early effort to work out an overall plan for your graduate program, you will be much better able to organize your work and to make intelligent decisions when changes need to be made in your program. A plan is essential for self-evaluation of your progress. Periodic attention to this plan, with appropriate revision, can significantly increase the probability of your succeeding in the graduate program. The plan will help you meet deadlines and identify activities most likely to be bottlenecks (and thus help you to anticipate work crunches). The plan will help you predict effects of deviations from schedule, such as getting sick, taking a vacation, or trying another experiment. While your overall goal may be to get a master's degree, you need a detailed series of interim goals whereby your progress and achievement can be measured as you go along and, perhaps even more important, to help you avoid unnecessary discouragement.

All thesis topics become predictably frayed, frustrating, and even boring at various times. Even with a project chosen because it interested you greatly, there will be times when you must remind yourself why you are doing what you are doing. You may, at times, even wonder why you are in graduate school at all. For this reason, psychologists suggest that it is better to attempt a lengthy or complicated project—like a thesis project—one chunk at a time rather than as a single undifferentiated whole.[7] You have a sense of accomplishment as intermediate goals are met. This builds confidence and adds to drive. Furthermore, difficulty with a single step is isolated, so it doesn't seem quite so overwhelming.

Discouragement

Several aspects of graduate school are highly conducive to discouragement, or general feelings of inadequacy. In starting graduate

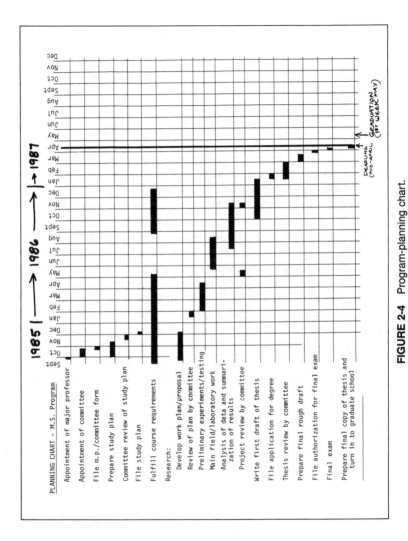

FIGURE 2-4 Program-planning chart.

school, the sudden lack of direction and criteria for success, and the change from undergraduate standards of performance based on working for grades in courses, often result in a sense of lost control and a continual falling short of one's expectations. While such problems cannot be avoided entirely, they can be greatly minimized with a little forethought.

A sense of lost control can overwhelm you when you cease to see clearly how what you are currently doing relates to your overall goal. Refer to your plan regularly, especially when you are getting discouraged. Have a clear set of research objectives as well. Any time—while gathering literature or data, reading, or analyzing—you feel that you are losing control of where you are and what it all means, *stop* and get yourself up to date psychologically. Take a significant portion of your time to sit down and reassess your progress, to tabulate your data, to jot down your questions and ideas. Keep a project record book and fill it with work summaries. Intersperse data collection with times to summarize. If you are running laboratory or field tests, schedule at least one day a week to summarize and write. Weekly summaries in your record book, carefully written progress reports (monthly or bimonthly) to your advisor, and regular meetings with your committee members will all benefit you in a measurable way. These activities will keep you on track and will reduce the severity of any periods of discouragement that you might encounter.

In addition to paying close attention to your work plan, you can at least do two other things to reduce discouragement and to enhance your success and enjoyment in the graduate program. First, develop realistic expectations. Second, recognize the necessity for flexibility and change in your work. Periodically check back to your overall plan and to your research objectives and modify them to make them more realistic. If you continually feel that you are not doing enough, your expectations are probably unrealistic. Having goals too far out of reach serves no useful purpose. Feeling guilty and inadequate saps your energy and takes the joy and focus out of your work.

Time Management
Being on schedule or even a little bit ahead of schedule is a sign of good planning and sound research effort. Successful planning and

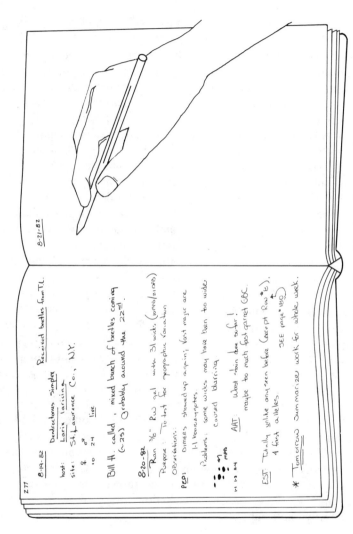

FIGURE 2-5 Record-book entries.

organization require intelligent use of time. A plan that looks good on paper, but which cannot be completed as scheduled, is not a very good plan. A good research or work plan is one that can be followed, one that has realistic and attainable deadlines. To make a good graduate program plan or a research plan with a realistic schedule requires some skill at estimating time. Most of us seriously underestimate the time tasks require and are disappointed with ourselves when a task takes longer than we had anticipated. We often feel that we have failed at the task when, in truth, all we failed at was estimating time. We might have done a good job at the task if we'd given ourselves a little more time. Such underestimation can result in a feeling of defeat, even if the work being accomplished is above average. Set fairly high standards, but ones you can reach with reasonable frequency. I was once advised to automatically multiply by two the time I expected a task to take. This works for me, although some people say multiplying by three works even better.

Start today to improve your time estimates. Take one simple task, such as making a trip to the library, doing an assignment, or reading a chapter, and estimate—*before* you do it—the amount of time you think it will take. Then do the task without hurrying, but working in a relatively efficient manner. You are not trying to beat the clock, merely trying to see how long the task really takes. If you find the task took longer than you expected (and it probably will), realize that you didn't fail to perform the task adequately, but that you failed to estimate realistically the time required. Each time you perform a task, try to estimate more accurately the actual time it will take. Don't continue to try to force your activities into unrealistic and discouragingly low time estimates. Once you begin to give yourself enough time to do things well, your day-to-day planning, efficiency, and satisfaction with your performance will improve noticeably.

Change

While planning is critical to the success of your program, keep in mind that all plans are tentative; all plans change. It is unrealistic and unproductive to view your initial work plan as a rigid scheme to follow. No matter how good you are at planning, the study plan that goes to the graduate school and your work plan or research proposal are only *estimates* of what you will do in the future. Changing your plan as you go along is expected and appropriate. Continually seek ways to modify and improve your plan. Because research involves looking for something new, there is no way that you can precisely plan how or even what you are going to discover. If you knew ahead of time exactly what you were looking for and how to find it, you would discover nothing very new or very important. If you are to acquire genuinely new knowledge, you will not know the answer in advance. Significant discoveries require us to go beyond the safe certainty of mechanistic research projects.[4] You must be ready, willing, and eager to take advantage of a clue, a new direction, or whatever it takes to facilitate the discovery process and reach your overall goal. No one on your committee or at the graduate school expects all your plans to be carried out with no change.

SELF-IMAGE

Another way that unrealistic expectations can manifest themselves is through the "impostor phenomenon."[5] Many college students, and especially graduate students, suffer from this condition. It is a gloomy and private feeling that someone will find you out. You secretly feel that any minute the world will discover that you're an incompetent fraud. It may be some relief to you to know that this feeling has virtually nothing to do with your actual competence but quite a lot to do with the disparity between your past experiences and your current situation. Students who are the first in their families to go to college or graduate school, and women in nontraditional fields, are particularly susceptible to this syndrome because their expectations are unrealistic or ill-defined. You might have nightmarish visions of your committee listening politely to a progress report and then asking, "Who are you trying to kid?" Fortunately, such feelings fade with experience and time as your self-image comes closer to reality.

Because graduate research is largely an independent effort, graduate students tend to become rather solitary. This behavior can exaggerate feelings of isolation, of uniqueness, of being out of place in graduate school. Keep in mind that you are not competing with other graduate students for a limited number of degrees. You are all in the same boat and experiencing many of the same feelings and difficulties. An effort to get to know other graduate students, professionally and socially, can significantly enhance your experience in graduate school. (Later on, these graduate students can form an important and useful network of professional contacts throughout the country.)

The emphasis on reading and writing may also alter your life toward a more sedentary pattern. Being out of shape is very bad for your self-image. As you must take time to interact with other students and with your advisor, also take time to exercise regularly. Being fit will improve your outlook and increase your stamina for the long days that research requires.

A FINAL WORD

While all of the activities mentioned above will help you avoid unnecessary discouragement, a general feeling of disenchantment (or angst) seems to settle upon many, if not most, graduate students during the later stages of their program. Students enter graduate school hoping to achieve some sort of personal and professional perfection. When they find such perfection lacking in their environment, they may become preoccupied and discouraged by the flaws they see in advisors, programs, policies, and departments. While each student or student group tends to think that these flaws are unique to their own situation, such feelings are virtually universal and relatively independent of the quality of the program. This angst is perhaps an inevitable part of learning to be an independent thinker. If not recognized as such, it can manifest itself in groups of graduate students in which complaining has been raised to recreational status.

Chapter 3

Getting Started

By choosing a general problem area to study, selecting an advisor and a graduate committee, and by working out an overall plan for your graduate program, you have already gotten a good start. This chapter deals with the specifics of getting started on the actual research project, defining and limiting the problem to be investigated, and preparing a written work plan.

CHOOSING A TOPIC

Contrary to myth, choice of a topic is not an inspirational point in time, but rather an extended process.[27] In the first phase, the student sorts out a list of possible topics. In the second phase, the student explores—through development of a written work plan or proposal—the feasibility, originality, and potential value of his or her first choice. The final decision upon a topic, however, ranges from one that is entirely the student's to one that is almost entirely the advisor's. In some cases, a professor has a grant and needs a student to work, as a research assistant, on part of it. This may be a good opportunity to develop a graduate research project, with the added benefit of financial support. Also, much of the groundwork (the literature search and problem definition) may already be done, and the research advisor may have great interest in seeing that the project proceeds rapidly and successfully.

Although this situation may seem ideal, it has a few potentially serious disadvantages. Just because a project has been developed by a professor and funded by a granting agency does not necessarily mean that the project is particularly good from a scientific standpoint or particularly appropriate, in terms of difficulty or duration, for a thesis project. In addition, a student handed a funded project based on an already written proposal is never forced to understand completely the questions that went into developing the problem. As a result, the student may not appreciate the answers as they are obtained. Skimming over the important early stages of the research process, and starting out with an emphasis on methods, can result in a serious lack of understanding of the research process as a whole. This weakness is often painfully evident at the preliminary examination or the final thesis defense.

Another disadvantage of undertaking part of an ongoing research project is that the student does not originate his or her own project. However, at the master's level, the student is expected mainly to gain an understanding of the research process. The level of originality demonstrated during the development of the project by the student is not as important as it is during a doctoral program. Thus, taking on an already-defined project (assuming it is in your general area of interest) might be quite acceptable, as long as an effort is made to thoroughly understand how the problem was developed. Even the constraints of a predefined project usually leave room for creativity. Because the basic purpose of graduate school is education, students offered a research assistantship linked to a particular project are usually given some flexibility and responsibility in developing their own objectives.

The other extreme occurs when a student has a particular research area in mind but is not able, or does not want, to become involved in research projects underway at the institution. If the student is self-supporting or finds financial assistance not related to a specific research project (such as teaching assistantship, a scholarship, or a college-awarded research assistantship or fellowship), the choice of project is basically up to the student. For this reason, a student working without a direct link to a funded research project has the potential advantage of developing a project tailored specifically to his or her own interests and talents. However, along with freedom of choice goes a greater responsibility for the success of the project itself and, often, the problem of personally generating funds to cover costs of equipment, photocopying, computer time, and travel.

In my experience, there does not seem to be a direct correlation between a student's source of funding or the amount of prior proposal writing by the professor and the quality of the student's finished thesis. Unless you have agreed to work on a funded project and are being paid specifically to do it, the choice of a research direction and of a project is yours. The advisor's role is to present information and opinions based on his or her greater experience, to help you choose among your options. Further, nearly any competent advisor will have, within his or her area of interest, a diversity of relevant topics to suggest for research projects. Explore these options. Your advisor can help you judge which projects are of sufficient depth, but which, at the same time, can be handled without undue difficulty and with the resources available. The project you choose should be one where you can do most of the work yourself. Profit from the advice you receive and attempt to work out a mutually interesting and beneficial project with your advisor.

Evaluating Your Choice

Regardless of how you arrived where you are now, it is safe to assume that you have a research topic in mind, even if it is as vague as, for example, to learn to model insect population dynamics, or to learn more about the effects of wildfires on forests. At this early stage, it is very important that you spend some time thinking about your choice of topic, since this project will take all of your days (and probably many of your nights) for the next 2 to 4 years. Seriously consider, on a very personal level, the following questions:

How does this topic fit your background and past experiences?

It may not. Maybe the reason you chose this topic was that you wanted a new direction.

How does this topic suit your interests? That is, how does it relate to what you like to do?

By now, with experiences in high school, college, and a diversity of outside activities, hobbies, and jobs, you should have some idea of what interests you. Good research usually results from an area in which you have a great deal of interest, from a topic about which you can periodically generate some excitement or enthusiasm. What do *you* like about this topic? How does it relate to what you most enjoy doing? Research can be designed to include many things that you like to do. If you love being outdoors, you could design a lot of field work into your study. If you enjoy tinkering with equipment, you might incorporate more laboratory work into your study. If you like computers, or want to learn more about them, design this into your project. There is more flexibility in this regard than you might realize at the outset.

How does this topic fit your career goals? How will it help you to be what you want to be as a professional at a future date?

Why do you think that information derived from research on this topic would be useful, interesting, or relevant to someone else?

This question has considerable survival value. If you wish to make a significant contribution with your research and/or to be paid to do it, now or in the future, it is important to choose a project that is useful, or at least interesting, to others. Nobel laureate Peter Medawar[21] says:

> [A]ny scientist of any age who *wants to make important discoveries must study important problems*. Dull or piffling problems yield dull or piffling answers. . . . [T]he problem must be such that it *matters* what the answer is—whether to science generally or to mankind. . . . [N]o young scientist need think that he will gain a reputation or high preferment merely by compiling information—particularly information of the kind nobody really wants. But if he makes the world more easily understandable by any means—whether theoretical or experimental—he will earn his colleagues' gratitude and respect.

If you draw a blank with more than one of these questions, you may have to seriously reevaluate your choice of a topic. Even a high level of funding for a project is not worth ignoring your interests and goals. You would not enjoy doing the research and you probably would not do a particularly good job at it. Now is the time to choose another topic, if a change seems warranted.

THE WORK PLAN

Once you have decided on a research topic, however general it may be at this stage, you should begin preparing a written work plan (also called a thesis proposal) for your project. The work plan is an exact statement of the problem you wish to investigate and the approach you propose to use in solving it. Writing it is the process by which you decide definitely upon a project. It is an extended, systematic exploration of the topic, and the end product must convince others that the project is appropriate and realistic. The plan forms an agreement with your committee about what you will do. It is usually prepared after considerable discussion with your advisor and submitted to your committee for review and approval. Working it through helps establish a goal-oriented pattern of relationships with your committee.

The work plan is linked to the final thesis in several very important ways. Writing itself is the key to this link. You must start

by translating the poorly understood to the well understood. A
technique can often be applied quickly and easily to a project, but
without theoretical depth, the thesis will not be outstanding.
Despite the best of intentions, you will overlook many important
aspects of your research, and research in general, if you do not
prepare a written work plan. Attempting to write clarifies your
ideas. You cannot write clearly without thinking clearly. And
having a written plan is the only way you and your advisors can
evaluate your progress, later on, in any concrete way. As
Woodford[30] pointed out:

> The power of writing as an aid in thinking is not often appreciated.
> Everyone knows that someone who writes successfully gets his
> thoughts completely in order before he publishes. But it is seldom
> pointed out that the very act of writing can help to clarify thinking.
> Put down woolly thoughts on paper, and their woolliness is immedi-
> ately exposed. If students come to realize this, they will write
> willingly and frequently at all stages of their work, instead of
> relegating "writing up" to the very end and regarding it as a dreadful
> chore that has very little to do with their "real" work.

Writing the thesis proposal or work plan may be as difficult as
writing the thesis itself. However, the plan is essential; there is
some evidence that most graduate students who don't complete
their degree programs are those who never worked out a plan with
their advisor and committee.[27] A proposal reviewed and accepted
by the committee is their vote of confidence in your project. Your
internalization of this confidence allows you to do your research
and write your thesis with less anxiety and self-doubt, particularly
if parts of the proposal have been written in thesis form.

Once the plan is written, preparation of progress reports
becomes a simple matter of checking to see where you should be at
a given time, then describing where you actually are, what
modifications of the program are appropriate, and what remains to
be done. All this is critically important when you get to the end of
the research project and begin to write your thesis.

You don't want to be (and you won't be) one of those
graduate students who spends 6 months attempting to write a
thesis and hating every minute of it because it is so difficult—being

blocked and wasting weeks with a desk covered with data but no idea where or how to begin writing. That situation is a classic result of doing research *wrong,* and it is why writing a work plan for your project is essential, regardless of whether your particular institution requires it. If you make an effort to write as you go along—a work plan and then project summaries or progress reports for your committee—writing the first complete draft of a master's thesis can be done in as little as a month and a Ph.D. thesis in perhaps two.

It may sound obvious to say you should start at the beginning, but this is what you must do. Methods are not the beginning. The beginning of the research process is the observation/problem-definition/hypothesis stage. Initial efforts at doing research include finding out what is known about your topic, identifying a gap in human understanding about that topic, and deciding what you are going to do to help fill that gap. In the introduction to your written work plan, you will include this information as a statement of the problem, your objectives, and background, or literature review (not necessarily in this order). Following the introduction is a methods section, which describes how you will carry out your objectives, and a timetable or schedule for completion. At some point, either in the introduction or perhaps following the methods section, your expected results and, most important, the value of the work should be described.

WORK PLAN OUTLINE

1 Introduction
   Background
   Problem statement
   Objectives
   Value of work
2 Methods
3 Timetable

When a work plan is written up as a grant proposal, a request for funding, the methods section is expanded to include a management plan. Sections detailing use of time, personnel, facilities, and money are added (see Chapter 4).

Before you start writing, however, you must begin to gather information and to think about how you will address the various components of the work plan. To do this, talk about your topic with your advisor, your committee members, and others. Gain appropriate preliminary experience in the field or laboratory, and start a literature search.

Because the testing procedures are often the most clear-cut part of the research, many reseachers (and not just graduate students) tend to focus almost exclusively upon developing their tests, or methods. When preliminary tests and tinkering with equipment are done as part of an attempt to pull ideas together and to gain needed experience, they can form an important part of the early stages of research. They help you think through the problem. But such activities can be a fatal flaw in the project if they shift your attention from developing a general understanding of the problem. Even if the overall project has already been developed and described, the literature search done, and the methods worked out, you will still need to go back and work through all of it yourself to begin to thoroughly understand the project and to be able to define, in concrete terms, what you will do.

Expect to spend 2 to 3 months completing the first rough draft of your work plan for review by your committee. This is not much time, especially when you also have a heavy load of coursework, but doing this early is an important part of getting started. Once you have completed the first draft, getting helpful feedback from your advisors and working to modify and improve it is much easier. Putting off writing the work plan does not make the writing easier later. It will only make you sorry that you procrastinated. You must suppress your embarrassment in revealing these first efforts to your advisor and others. Writing well takes a great deal of practice, so your first efforts may seem rather crude. Your advisors will be looking for *improvement* of the plan, your writing, and the adequacy of your responses to their suggestions. Expecting perfection of yourself, or even expecting to be satisfied with your initial efforts, is unrealistic. Writing is a learned skill, like painting a picture or shooting a basketball. The only way you can get good at it is to practice and to solicit—and use—criticism.

One good approach is to write and edit a draft of a section of the work plan, then give it to your advisor or someone else for feedback. When you get the draft back, you will feel ready to go at it again with fresh enthusiasm and insight. (Throughout your research, you should try to write parts of your research report—methods or ideas for discussion, for example—as you go along, when ideas and details are fresh in your mind. Later, the job of tying the parts together for the first draft of your thesis will be comparatively easy.)

The Literature Search

A literature search can be viewed as two separate processes, the intellectual and the logistic. The intellectual part has to do with the generation of ideas and the synthesis of information. It consists of reading and thinking about the research area; attempting to formulate, while doing so, the key questions; defining a specific problem to work on; and developing testable hypotheses. It also involves acquiring a broad knowledge of the subject of your research and related subjects. The logistic part involves all the organizational or mechanical aspects of acquiring information—learning to use the library at your school, acquiring pertinent articles and books, and developing some useful system of keeping your lists of references and notes. The more efficient the system you develop for collecting and organizing references and notes, the freer your mind will be to devote to the actual research problem.

A literature search is a continuous, never-ending process, not something done during only one stage of the research. New literature keeps appearing and, even if you keep meticulously up to-date, someone can always point out a relevant article that you missed. In the beginning, each paper you read can lead to several others, so don't expect, or even try, to complete a literature search before moving on to the next stage in your research. Focus on the literature for a while—perhaps for a few weeks—and then start writing.

Many graduate students envision the literature search to be a very systematic process, a sort of careful sweep of the literature starting at Year 1 and working methodically through to the current year. This approach may be useful during later stages of your research, but it is not the best way to start. The main thing you need to do in the beginning is to get a general grasp of the area and to begin focusing your questions. At this early stage, you don't need, or want, to get bogged down in detail.

Start by obtaining a few important articles in your subject area, and perhaps a recent review article or book suggested by your advisor and others in your research area. In reading these, note ideas and seemingly useful references from the bibliographies. Within a very short time, you will have quite a number of references and will begin to grasp some of the fundamental problems and questions that your research might address. As you read these first few main articles, make a list of key words or phrases to use later, when you get to the more systematic and thorough aspects of a literature review. Key words might include taxonomic designations (such as species names) and topic words (such as turbulence or melanization).

Once you have obtained a good representation of the main papers in your topic and have read them and taken time to assimilate the information, begin writing. In approaching the literature search this way, you will avoid or minimize what Eisenberg[12] calls "data poisoning." Data poisoning occurs when the background information becomes unwieldy, when you have too much information to assimilate at one time. This stage will arrive much sooner than you expect. Try to stop gathering information before you are overwhelmed with it, and write. Break up your reading and writing with field or laboratory work and brief discussions with others, giving your brain time to absorb and integrate ideas. If you find yourself overwhelmed and confused, pick out only a few main references and write from them. Other information can be incorporated later.

Your literature review can be written in one of two ways: by authors or by ideas. In the first, the history of a research area is given by describing what individual people did, in chronological order—for example, "In 1946, Johnson found that Smith's (1937) conclusions did not apply in situations where. . . ." The second approach—development of ideas—is, in my view, much better. This approach focuses on the development of a conceptual basis for understanding an area, leading up to the present. "Observations of . . . led to greater understanding of changes in . . . (Johnson 1946)." Authors of important research are treated as secondary to the ideas they developed. Once you start writing from the literature, the difference between these two styles will become clearer to you.

No one expects the first literature review you write to be complete. For this reason, a word-processing facility is very helpful in research writing because you can add and change as you go along, with minimum retyping. Most university computers now have a word-processing capability. If you don't have your own personal computer, ask your advisor or someone at the computer center how you might get an account (if one is needed) for word processing, and then learn to word process. In most institutions, the entire thesis, including the final draft, can now be done on the computer.

It is helpful to keep in mind that all wisdom is not contained in the literature. In fact, some knowledgeable researchers argue *against* study of the literature before undertaking a research project. By studying the literature and learning what others have done, you subconsciously learn how an area has *not* been approached, and, regrettably, may develop a certain inability to see the research area in a new or innovative way. In any case, it is vitally important that you read critically. According to Medawar:[21]

> The number and complexity of the techniques and supporting disciplines used in research are so large that a novice may easily be frightened into postponing research in order to carry on with the process of "equipping himself." As there is no knowing in advance where a research enterprise may lead and what kinds of skills it will require as it unfolds, this process of "equipping oneself" has no predetermined limits and is bad psychological policy, anyway; we always need to know and understand a great deal more than we do already and to master many more skills than we now possess. The great incentive to learning a new skill or supporting discipline is an urgent need to use it. For this reason, very many scientists (I certainly among them) do not learn new skills or master new disciplines until the pressure is upon them to do so; thereupon they can be mastered pretty quickly. . . . Very similar considerations

apply to a novice's inclination to spend weeks or months "mastering the literature." Too much book learning may crab and confine the imagination, and endless poring over the research of others is sometimes psychologically a research substitute, much as reading romantic fiction may be a substitute for real-life romance. . . . The beginner *must* read, but intently and choosily and not too much.

All published research is not equally well done, and all articles are not equally useful. Some work is just plain poor, even some papers appearing in the most prestigious journals. Use your judgment as to which articles may be most helpful. For example, in selecting methods to use, don't assume a method is the right one to use just because someone else used it before you. The V technique, described later in this chapter, is extremely useful for evaluating research articles and theses for your literature review. The V can also help you distinguish between, and assess the validity of, factual statements and speculations or generalizations made by other researchers.

Two items useful in organizing the literature review, and your research in general, are a record book and a card file. The importance of complete and accurate records for your research, and especially for writing your thesis, cannot be overemphasized. A record book is used something like a diary, a place where you keep information on your research as it progresses. The record book can be particularly useful in the library because, while there, you often stop for one reason or other in the middle of some task. Having a record book with you means you can jot down just where you were when you left off and perhaps what you need to do next time. Many students use a hardbound $7\frac{1}{2} \times 9\frac{3}{4}$ inch account or ledger book. These are fairly expensive but one or two may be sufficient for an entire project. They have the advantages of being string-bound so that pages won't fall out, they open flat, and pages are numbered so you can cross-reference items. For some projects, however, a loose-leaf notebook is more convenient.

In your record book or some other central location, keep detailed accounts of everything you do or that happens related to your research. The sooner you begin to develop this habit the better. It is not easy to remember in April just which of the

November tests was done with buffer A and which with buffer B, or when you switched to technique X. Try to write in your record book nearly every day, and date each entry. Tape into it all those bits of paper with names, phone numbers, addresses, and messages that are pertinent, or potentially pertinent, to your research project. Write in it reminders to yourself, questions, ideas, lists, and periodic summaries of progress. Store it in a central location with photocopies of important articles, photographs, computer output, and other items related to your research.

You will also need to keep orderly reference lists. One way to do this is to carry a packet of 3 × 5 inch lined file cards. Each time you find a pertinent reference, fill out a complete reference card as shown in Figure 3-1. Find out the format required for bibliographies in theses at your institution. (Your department office probably has a supply of recently completed master's and doctoral theses that you can inspect.) Transcribe all references in this format so you don't have to go back a second time to pick up information you missed. Avoid abbreviations as much as possible. You might forget what they mean. Taking complete citations and making reference cards is time-consuming but you'll be glad you did it. When it comes time to write your bibliography, all you will have to do is sort the cards you made into alphabetic order and start writing.

Periodically, file your cards in a box in your office and, if you are using a word processor, update your reference list. At the same time you are collecting cards, start collecting your own copies of good references to annotate for your own purposes. This is worth paying for yourself, but your advisor may be able to help with copying costs through his or her research budget.

In starting a literature search, you will usually look at books, review articles, and journals with original research in your subject area. Some of the articles may be many years old. While literature cited in these articles enables you to move backward in time to earlier articles of interest, the *Science Citation Index* enables you to move forward in the literature to about six months behind the latest articles. If you have an important but not very recent paper in your area, you can use the Science Citation Index to quickly find

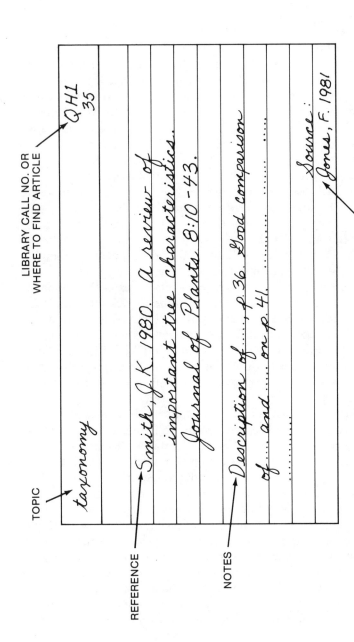

TOPIC

LIBRARY CALL NO. OR
WHERE TO FIND ARTICLE

REFERENCE

NOTES

SOURCE OF REFERENCE

FIGURE 3-1 Reference card.

out who has cited that paper in more current research publications.

After you have read some of the main papers, roughed out your written introduction to the work plan, and gotten a better idea of what you are looking for, you may want to attempt a systematic literature search. Having done some reading, you will know what key words to use and approximately how far back in the literature you may have to search. In some areas, papers relevant to the project may have appeared 50 to 100 years ago. In others, nothing was done until more recently. This is something you will begin to get a feel for in your initial readings.

Your systematic literature review may include a computer search and/or a manual search through the major abstracting references. Most libraries offer computer searches, usually at cost. Whether such a search would be useful for you depends on a number of factors. Computer searches work best for concrete, well-defined topics. You will have to explain to the search analyst exactly what you're looking for, which is one good reason for not starting out with this approach. Costs for a computer search include a computer-time charge for using the data base and a per-item cost for printing. Total cost is generally related to the size of the topic—how long it takes to enter the concepts and search for them, and the number of items retrieved. An average search costs less than $100.

Is it worth it? Consider that a 10-minute search can scan an index that might take you several days to cover thoroughly by hand. Also, the computer searches not only key words from the title and index terms, but the abstracts as well. And the terms can be combined and limited in ways not possible when doing a manual search. However, most data bases for computer searches go back only 10 to 15 years, so if you must go back further than that, you'll still end up searching much of the literature manually.

The key to an efficient manual search is picking the right indexes and attacking each of them in the way most appropriate to that index. Talk it over with the local librarian. Librarians are there to help you. Ask for their help frequently. There are literally hundreds of indexing and abstracting services, each with its own peculiar characteristics and coverages. Getting advice before starting any literature search can save you many frustrating hours.

Obtaining Current Information

Even a thorough literature search must not be considered a way to know completely either what has been studied in your area or what is currently going on. The most recently published articles, particularly material that appears in books or in reviewed (refereed) journals, are at least 2 years out of date. To understand this time lag and the problems associated with getting really current information, you should have some idea of the chronology of publication. The following example itemizes steps and time involved in a typical publication:

Data collected, summer 1985

Data analyzed and interpreted and manuscript written, fall 1985

Manuscript sent to colleagues for review, winter 1985–86

Manuscript revised and submitted to journal, April 1986

Manuscript sent to reviewers by journal editor and returned to author for revision (2 to 6 months), August 1986

Manuscript revised and returned to journal, September 1986

Manuscript appears in print (3 to 18 months later), May 1987

This whole process has taken nearly 2 years, and it would have taken longer if everything had not gone smoothly. In this example, the paper was written soon after the research was done and the manuscript was not rejected from one or more journals. The published paper appears in the abstracting journal about 6 to 9 months later. It is thus incorrect to believe that the literature contains a current record of what is going on in your field.

Other erroneous beliefs are that a search of an abstracting journal in your field constitutes a thorough search of the literature and that all research results are published. You can perhaps more correctly assume that, at best, much less than half of research appears in published articles. All researchers have, to a greater or lesser extent, a backlog of publishable material that got sidelined.

How *do* you find current information? It is vital to identify and contact others doing research in your area, wherever they might be. Write to the authors of some of the most useful articles in your subject area (addresses are always given on the title page of a journal article) and ask them what they are doing. Many will not answer, but others will send you unpublished reports or manuscripts which can be exceedingly helpful. Some will pass your letter on to one of their graduate students, through whom you can often find out more about what is going on in that particular group than you can through the senior researcher. If your advisor or other faculty members in your department are well-established in a particular area, they probably keep up-to-date by reviewing manuscripts of their colleagues and will have a good idea of who is doing what right now. Some advisors share their reviewing duties with their graduate students, giving the students a chance both to keep up-to-date and to gain reviewing experience.

An excellent source of detailed and up-to-date information is recent theses, obtainable through your library's holdings, the interlibrary loan system, or directly from the student or his or her major professor. Copies of Ph.D. theses can be bought for about $30 from University Microfilms (in Ann Arbor, Michigan; the toll-free telephone number is 800/521-3042). Even if they are not particularly recent, theses often provide more detailed information, especially on methods, than ever appears in the published literature, and they often include raw data that can be reanalyzed in new ways.

Society Memberships

Be sure to join one or more of the main professional societies in your area of interest. If a particular society requires that you be nominated for membership, ask someone (such as your advisor) to nominate you. Membership is usually not expensive (nearly all have much-reduced student rates) and it serves a number of purposes. Membership often includes a subscription to an important journal. For example, membership in the Society of American Foresters gets you the *Journal of Forestry*. Members of Sigma Xi get *The American Scientist*.

Even more important, as a society member, you get information about annual regional and national professional meetings in your area of interest, and meetings are one of the keys to keeping current in research. There you can hear presentations detailing current research and ideas that may be years away from appearing in the literature, and meet and talk with others doing similar work. There is much time for informal small group or one-to-one discussion in a relaxed setting. Many of the most valuable contacts at meetings are made in this way. You will find that many of the researchers whose work you have read and admired are helpful and interested in your own project when you meet them face to face. Follow up these meetings with letters to reemphasize your interest in their work and to help ensure that they remember who you are. After you have met or spoken to some of these people, it is much easier to write to them or call them on the phone, or to talk to their graduate students. Enough cannot be said about the value of professional meetings. They are worth a great effort to find out about and to attend.

Besides helping you keep current in your field, professional meetings can stimulate your thinking in productive ways. Significant research is an outcome of investigator activity and exposure.[4] Researchers who do research based solely on the next logical step from a recent journal article are less likely to achieve something outstanding. Frequent interactions with other researchers, as well as with the users of research results, are the source of good research ideas. Medawar[21] says, "Isolation is disagreeable and bad for graduate students. The need to avoid it is one of the best arguments for joining some intellectually bustling concern." Even if you find your department, college, or university is a relatively satisfying center of "intellectual bustle," making contacts outside of your own institution creates a broader and even more useful network of intellectual activity and stimulation.

As you meet and correspond with other researchers, communicate openly about your work. Share ideas, proposals, and manuscripts. Being secretive has few, if any, benefits for your work. The risk that someone will steal your ideas is much smaller than the benefits received from developing an open and mutually helpful network of professional contacts. According to Medawar:[21]

> Secretiveness in a scientist is a disfigurement. . . . [O]ne of the most comically endearing traits of a young research worker is the illusion

that everyone else is eager to hurry off to do his research before he can. . . . A scientist who is too cagey or suspicious to tell his colleagues anything will soon find that he himself learns nothing in return.

Because of the importance of professional meetings, an added benefit of society membership is that it looks very good on your résumé. Societies are viewed favorably by those reviewing you for scholarships or jobs. Membership in professional societies indicates to others that you are at least aware that there are others in your field and are probably aware of current research in this area. It is, of course, assumed that if you are a society member you are active, to some extent, in the society.

PROBLEM DEFINITION

Problem definition requires focusing all the general background information into a specific graduate research project. Good research begins with disorder but ends with order.[4] Logic and certainty do not begin the process, but are an outcome of the process. From the information you gather from the literature and from discussing and working on your topic with your advisors, a problem that interests you should begin to emerge. You will see many gaps in the information available or places where knowledge gives way to uncertainty. Try writing the research problem down as a question or questions and then formulate some hypotheses—guesses—about what you think the answers might be. From these hypotheses will come your objectives (what you will do to help answer the question) and methods (how you will carry out your objectives).

In working to identify a graduate research project, you will soon become aware that there is no way to address the entire problem or set of problems that exist within your topic. This is true no matter how hard-working and intelligent you may be. Fortunately, you are not expected to solve the entire problem. Once the overall problem is defined, you must set boundaries around the portion of it that you will address in your research. This process of setting limits on your research is much like building fences around property. A lot of practical considerations—time, effort, finances —go into deciding just where the fences should go. In spite of obvious logistical constraints, it is often very hard to make these decisions, and your first effort at problem definition, at developing a set of questions, hypotheses, and objectives, will probably be much too broad. Going from the general problem to a research project that you can do effectively is always difficult, and it is most difficult the first time you do it. This is because there are, in fact, no real boundaries on research projects, only boundaries that you artificially impose. Setting these boundaries can seem, at first, a very frustrating experience. And the more curious, motivated, and intelligent you are, the more you will see the artificiality of these boundaries and tend, at first, to bite off more than you can chew. Everything you do in your research will lead to something else. Every question answered will lead to a hundred more interesting questions.

The same arbitrary limits must be set to terminate your project and to write your thesis. Setting a completion date in the first planning stages of your graduate program will help you do this. When that date draws near, you just start writing your thesis in earnest. At no point will the research seem truly complete and finished. It can be very discouraging and frustrating if you expect it to be.

HYPOTHESES

Hypotheses—your guesses as to what your research will show— must be testable in a specific way. In working out your hypotheses, ask yourself if each hypothesis, as stated, leads clearly to a manageable test that will provide useful results. Is the hypothesis too broad or too narrow, or off the point? Avoid using vague terms, such as "environmental factors" or "chemical composition," unless you qualify them (for example, ". . . key environmental factors: rainfall, insolation, and temperature"). If you aren't sure how to state your hypotheses more specifically, check further in the literature and talk with your advisors to help get ideas. And plan to do a few preliminary experiments to help you decide on a limited number of variables to examine. For example, your stated question might be, "How does mineral nutrition of trees affect their susceptibility to insect infestation?" Your first hypothesis might be, "Inadequate mineral nutrition is related to higher levels of insect infestation." However, when you think ahead to the test that this implies, you will see that this hypothesis is much too broad. To test it, you must examine all tree species, all nutrients in all tree tissues, and infestation by all possible insects all over the world. Obviously, this is not what you intend to do. So you go back and restate the question more precisely as, perhaps, "Does the level of nitrogen and calcium in mature needles affect lodgepole pine's susceptibility to attack by the western needle miner in northern Idaho?" Now that's a little better. The hypotheses might be, "(1) Nitrogen and calcium levels in lodgepole pine needles vary among stands, and (2) Needle nitrogen and calcium levels are inversely correlated with infestation of lodgepole pine by the western needle miner." You might then do some work and realize that you just won't have time to look at both minerals and will limit your work to only one. Broad, general hypotheses are undesirable because they lead to broad, general objectives that do not focus the work in any useful or realistic way.

Although the word "hypothesis" sounds rather important and scientific, don't forget that it is only a guess. At this stage in your work, your hypotheses will be, at best, only semieducated guesses and, at worst, wild stabs in the dark. And most hypotheses turn out to be wrong. So once your hypotheses are stated, you must suppress, as best you can, your desire to be right, since this desire, human as it may be, interferes with the research process. The intensity of the conviction that a hypothesis is true has no bearing on whether it is true.[21]

On a practical level, develop the best tests you can to determine if your hypotheses are wrong. The soundest research discoveries are those where the researchers made great efforts to falsify their hypotheses. A researcher must be the most rigorous critic of his or her own ideas. Cherished beliefs not subjected to well-designed tests, and attempts to establish territories, by presenting methods or conclusions that no one else can replicate, have no place in research. Realizing early in your research that most initial hypotheses are wrong prepares you to seek ways to modify your own hypotheses and to accept the test results that present themselves as the research unfolds. Keep in mind that all testing is criticism.[21] If a test does not hold the possibility of causing you to revise your views, it is probably a poor test.

Statistical tests are designed to keep you honest in this respect. Your hypothesis is usually that there *is* a difference between A and B or that A *has* an effect on B. The null hypothesis in the statistical test is that there is no difference or effect, and your hypothesis becomes the alternative hypothesis. Unless you can then demonstrate a difference, you must accept the null hypothesis of no difference. It's like the "innocent till proven guilty" maxim in criminal law.

For each question you are asking in your research, work out one or more hypotheses. Examine your reasons for believing, at this point in your work, that this hypothesis might be correct. Then consider alternative hypotheses. What do these imply in terms of the significance of your work? That is, what if your testing provides evidence (and it very well may) that your original hypotheses are *not* correct? What value will your work have then?

OBJECTIVES

For each hypothesis, you will develop one or more objectives that tell what you will actually do to test the hypothesis. Your objectives define the limits of the proposed study: what will and what will not be covered. Each objective should add information to the preceding objective. The hypotheses stated above, for example, could lead to the following objectives:

1 Identify the range of variation of nitrogen and calcium in lodgepole pine needles in 10 stands selected to represent a range of soil nutrient levels and moisture conditions in northern Idaho.

2 Select lodgepole pine stands—two each with high, medium, low, and no infestation by the western needle miner—and determine levels of calcium and nitrogen in the needles of four trees in each stand.

A final objective should be included to say what you will do with all the information that you gather. For example:

3 Determine if any correlation exists between needle calcium or nitrogen levels and the level of western needle miner infestation in the test trees.

Evaluating Your Objectives

Several questions can be asked to judge the quality of your objectives. Perhaps the most important is: *Are these objectives realistic?* More than just about anything else, a realistic set of objectives is critical to the success of your project. Conversely, unrealistic objectives are one of the most serious flaws in a work plan. Hypotheses and objectives, carefully constructed, can proliferate faster than gerbils. Limit them to what you think you can realistically accomplish within the time period you have allotted for your graduate program.

It may help to think of objectives as being of three different kinds: (1) those you know you can easily accomplish, (2) those you should be able to do if all goes reasonably well, and (3) those you might be able to do if you work very hard and are very lucky. In your work plan, include objectives of the first two kinds. Objectives of the third kind might best be kept up your sleeve and not built into the program at the start (like extra courses in your study plan).

You are not expected to always accomplish everything you set out to do, but you should aim to do all of it. Nearly all beginning researchers tend to think they can accomplish more than they actually can in a given time period. If you are advised that your objectives are too extensive or that they are unrealistic in any way, given the scope of your graduate program, try to listen and benefit from the experience of others.

You should also ask yourself, *does each objective lead directly to a clear set of methods?* Each objective should be directly translatable into action (methods) with minimum ambiguity. Objectives form an outline of your methods. Once objectives are well defined, it is easy to plan and write up methods to carry them out in a logical way. If you find it difficult to write the methods section of your work plan, perhaps you need to go back and rework your objectives.

Do these objectives form a solid foundation for future work in this area? Remember that you don't have to solve the entire problem. Indeed, you probably can't, even given a lifetime to do it. Objectives are your way of saying, "This is the *part* of the problem I am going to study" or "This is the way I am going to *start* working toward solution of the problem." Conceive of your objectives as some of the first steps toward a solution to the main question, a part that can eventually be fit together, like a puzzle piece, to help make the big picture. Focus on developing hypotheses and objectives that will help later researchers build upon your work and go further in this area.

Will each objective, by itself, provide useful information relevant to the central problem? While each objective builds on the one before it, try to make each of some value by itself. This helps ensure your success in research, because even if you don't finish all the objectives, you will still have discovered something of interest and value and will be able to write a thesis. As a corollary to this, ask yourself, *will each objective provide useful information regardless of whether the hypothesis upon which it was based was right or wrong?* Avoid stating objectives in a way that restricts you to finding results of only one kind—results that support your hypothesis—or failing. Examples of poor objectives might be, "To detect a correlation between A and B" or "To show [or prove] that method A is superior to method B for detecting. . . ."

Objectives provide a means by which you can continually review and evaluate your progress in your research project. They are your criteria for performance and accomplishment. However, they are subject to the same process of constant revision and refinement that is an integral part of all steps in the research process. Identifying a set of objectives at this point does not require that you follow them all rigidly. Each time you evaluate your progress, you might have to add or drop objectives, or at least refine or reword some of them. You might even find that you will need to restate your overall problem and questions into more specific and realistic terms.

METHODS

Your objectives form a transition from the introduction to the methods, from ideas to action. Once worked out, they form an outline for writing your methods. Each objective requires a separate set of methods, each building upon the previous one. As you develop your hypotheses, weigh different approaches to testing them. In the work plan, justify your choice of approaches, perhaps with a description of preliminary experiments.

Methods are usually divided into two major sections. The first is a description of what and how data are to be collected. The second part tells what you will do with the data once you get it, so that you can interpret it. This second part is often called analysis. In the outline below, methods are divided into data collection and data analysis. At this point in your research project, methods are written in the future tense. In writing the thesis, however, methods are past history and, accordingly, are written in the past tense.

According to the rational model of research, the type of problem should determine the choice of the most appropriate research methods. In reality, researchers tend to use the methods familiar to them. For obvious practical reasons, graduate students tend to choose methods familiar to their advisors. Such methods may or may not be optimal for your project. A desirable and often essential way to get unbiased answers to your research questions is to use more than one approach. If possible, incorporate an alternative method into your tests. Even if you are trying a totally new technique on an old problem, incorporation of a second approach can help ensure the objectivity of your findings. Adding another perspective will help you interpret your results more easily and will broaden your training in important ways. Overspecialization is a trap that catches many researchers at an early age. Your goal is not to become the world's authority on some minute aspect of your specialty area.

Early in the planning stages of your work, begin to keep a running record of all your cooperators—all who provided advice, supplies, pertinent references, access to equipment or special facilities, and so on. If this record is not started early, it is virtually impossible to remember at the end of your program when you must write the acknowledgments section of your thesis.

From the very beginning of your project, make a concentrated effort to take photographs (color slides are best) of all aspects of your work—laboratory setups, special techniques, field sites, and so on. If you don't have a camera, your advisor may have one that you can borrow or can suggest where you might borrow one. Photographs will be very important to you later on in writing the thesis and, more important, in adding interest to talks you give about your research. But appropriate photographs are difficult, and often impossible, to acquire at the last minute. Also, copy and file useful diagrams and illustrations (with complete reference citations written on them) from the work of others. If someone else shows a good slide of something in your topic area, ask permission to make a duplicate.

OUTLINING THE WORK PLAN

An excellent technique for outlining your project in a way that will help you organize and interrelate all the events, facts, and concepts you are using is the V^{13} (Figure 3-2). This technique is useful for thinking about, communicating, and evaluating research at any stage—from developing a research proposal to evaluating published research. The V is particularly helpful at this early stage of project development. As you read through the following section, sketch out a V of your project.

Questions and Central Event

To approach putting your project on a V, first identify the central event of the project and write it below the point of a V that you have drawn on a blank piece of paper. The central event is the particular portion of the world upon which you will focus your attention. The central event is often the title of the project. Examples of central events might be "Electrophoretic character-ization of six *Dendroctonus* species" or "Hunter attitudes toward road use policies in Idaho."

Next, consider the key question or questions that you will address. Write these in the middle of the broad upper part of the V. These questions should be concise and addressed specifically by your central event. One way to write these questions is to list one simple broad question and, under it, two or three specific questions relating directly to your project.

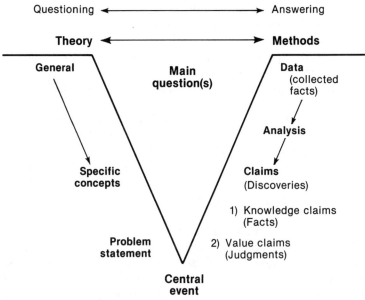

FIGURE 3-2 V-outline format.

Left Side of the V—Theory

The left side of the V tells how you arrived at the main questions and why you will be "doing" the central event. It is helpful to approach this from the perspective of what you would have to tell another person before he or she could understand why you are doing the particular project.

The left side of the V is important in both a theoretical and a practical way. You couldn't simply arrive at graduate school and go out and do your central event effectively. (Actually, you could, but you wouldn't have any real idea of what you were doing.) A lot of thinking and experience occurred before you could ask that question. Similarly, a lot of fundamental concepts (background information or theory) must be made clear before another person can understand why you will do the particular research. On the left side of the V, write down—from general (top) to more specific (bottom)—all the concepts that must be communicated before the reader can appreciate the problem. But don't trace the history of environmental pollution since the earth was formed, or the theory of combustion from the time two sticks were first rubbed together. Pertinent concepts might include mineral requirements of animals or height-diameter relationships in trees.

In listing concepts, difficulties arise in deciding which can be assumed to be generally known and which must be explained before another person can understand the research. What background and education can be expected of the reader of a research proposal, thesis, or research report? Students making their first attempt at writing about research nearly always assume too much of the reader and, in providing what they feel is relevant background information, require great leaps of the reader's imagination.

In your initial attempts at working out the left side of the V, try to err on the side of too much explanation, not too little. This way, you will probably come closer to providing adequate background in your first writing attempts. In a research proposal or thesis, you will not be writing for only your advisor or the two or three other people who are doing nearly the same kind of work as you are. Consider, for example, the outside person on your graduate committee. Even if you can assume that most of your readers work in the same general area as you do, it is necessary to refresh their memories and to define words that may not be clear. It is often best to assume that your intended reader is no more familiar with the problem than you were when you started the project. For example, although it may not be necessary to include "algebra" in your list of concepts, it may be necessary to include "development and use of wood volume equations." In general, readers like to read something they understand. Unless there is nothing new in the entire report, they do not feel that their intelligence is being insulted or their background underestimated. You know yourself that if you go to a class where some of the background on the day's subject is familiar to you, you feel good about both the teacher and the subject, and you learn something. When a teacher assumes you know more than you do when the subject is introduced, much of the value of the lecture is lost.

Be sure to include the concepts that you consider inadequately understood, since this provides a clear rationale for asking the questions and doing the research. End the left side of the V with a problem statement or a description of the deficiencies or lack of knowledge in the particular area that you address in your research.

Right Side of the V—Methods

The right side of the V tells how you will go about answering your questions and, at this stage in development of your project, what you expect to find. The central event implies a test approach, an experimental design. From this will come some sort of facts or data that you need to collect—raw data that you collect personally (such as costs, tree diameter measurements, or questionnaire results) and/or data collected by others (such as literature records, information from earlier theses, or maps). Data are bits of information which, by themselves, have little meaning.

Next consider how you will analyze these data so that they make sense to you and so that interpretations are possible. The simplest example of an analysis is a sum or average or percent taken from a series of data points. Equations, models, statistical tests, and special computer programs are also analyses. Development of a model can be an analysis or, if it is the real focus of your research, it can be the central event. Although data analysis may seem far in the future to you right now, you must start thinking, in specific terms, of how you will do it.

A researcher must also consider, from the very beginning of the project, how the work might be interpreted, what the possible outcomes might be. You have already done this in developing your hypothesis or hypotheses. On the V, these results and their interpretation (actual or potential) are listed as *claims*. At the end of your project, you will have made some discoveries of a factual nature and will be able to state these as *knowledge claims*. You might, for example, be able to say that a particular method is more accurate than another method under certain conditions but not others, or that summer burning costs are higher than spring or fall burning costs, or that high concentrations of iodophore result in increased mortality of young trout.

Other important outcomes of your research are the judgments and generalizations you make about the value of your results to others, the *value claims*. Value claims describe the extent to which you feel that your research results usefully fill a gap in human knowledge and what the broader applications of your findings might be. They go beyond a strict factual interpretation of the data. Value claims might also include what you believe needs to be done next or how the work should be done differently next time. To others, value claims are often the most useful outcomes of your research.

Relationship between the V and the Work Plan

Nearly all parts of the V can be included in your work plan (see Figures 3-3, 3-4, and 3-5). Concepts are presented in a logical and complete way, leading up to your questions or problem statement. This is followed by a description of the general approach you will use to answer these questions, a list of specific objectives, and a description of what you expect to find and what value the work will have.

In the methods section of your work plan, you expand upon your approach, discussing in detail your test design, and the specific way that you will address each objective, obtaining and analyzing the data in order to answer the research questions.

If you can put your project on a V, even in rudimentary form, you will be able to begin writing about your research in an organized way and, perhaps more important, you will be able to talk coherently to others about your project and to seek further information and ideas in a specific and maximally helpful manner. The V provides a framework for sorting out new bits of information as they are acquired and for filling out aspects of your project that are not well developed.

Once involved in a research project, most people find the right side of the V easiest to fill in. In fact, when research is not developed in a careful and well thought out way, it can stay heavy on methods. A major deficiency of much completed (and published) research is that the concepts have not been thought through in any systematic fashion. For graduate students, this deficiency is often painfully manifested during the preliminary

THEORY

Certain cultivars of apple bear fruit productively only every other year.

Gibberellins (GA) appear to have an inhibitory effect on floral initiation in some plants.

Gibberellins are commonly synthesized in young leaves of plants and are also present in developing seeds and fruit.

Concepts:

apple (Malus domestica)
cultivar
fruiting spur
floral initiation
biennial bearing
plant growth hormones
gibberellin (GA)
promalin

Problem:

Gibberellin sprays are currently being used on 'Red Delicious' apples to improve fruit shape. The mechanisms and degree of GA involvement in floral initiation of apple needs to be investigated further to determine the effect that exogenous GA applications might have on biennial bearing cycles.

Site(s) of gibberellin
Synthesis that contribute
to biennial bearing in
apple

1. What are endogenous levels of GA in apple tissues (leaves, spur leaves, seeds, and fruit) at the time of floral initiation?

2. How does the GA level in these apple tissues change with GA application?

3. Is there an increased inhibitory effect on floral initiation with GA application?

4. What is the critical level of gibberellin that inhibits floral initiation?

5. Is the amount of GA present in the spur leaves sufficient to contribute to inhib- ition of floral buds in apples?

METHODS

Data:

-levels of GA in apple tissues (leaves, spur leaves, seeds, fruit) of untreated plants.

-levels of GA in these tissues after GA_{4+7} appli- cations.

-GA levels in samples of plants sprayed at different times or with different concentrations of GA

-number of return bloom spurs

Analysis: An analysis of variance will be run and findings will be evaluated using Tukey's, Sheffe's, and Duncan's Multiple Range tests to determine the effect of treatments.

Hypotheses:

Knowledge Claim: The concentration of GA in the spur leaves is sufficient to contribute to inhibition of flowering in 'Delicious' apple.

Value Claim:

The results of this study will add to our understanding of biennial bearing in apple. A solution to this problem is important to fruit growers who seek a stabilized, uniform crop every year.

FIGURE 3-3 Work-plan outline—horticulture.

THEORY

-description of corona
 discharges
-corona-fluid coupling: space
 charge, corona wind
-corona-particle coupling:
 particle charging, coulombic
 force
-fluid-particle coupling: viscous
 drag, turbulent dispersion

Applications

-particulate collection: electro-
 static precipitators (ESPs)
-enhanced convective heat transfer
-electrogasdynamic power generation

Specific Concepts

Corona wind velocity is proportional to
 ion current; can exceed 2 m/s.
Corona wind is strongly affected by ambient
 gas flow.
Corona wind in ESPs exists as a turbulent,
 recirculating flow.
Corona wind pattern depends upon electrode
 geometry and polarity.
Particle motion is affected by corona wind
 through convection and turbulent dispersion.

Problem Statements

Turbulent nature of corona wind is poorly understood.
Parametric scaling laws for corona
 wind are unknown.
Corona wind effect on particle
 motion has not been experiment-
 ally isolated and measured.
The net effect of corona wind particle transport on
 ESP performance has not been established.

QUESTIONS

1) How do the following parameters affect the
 convective and turbulent nature of corona-
 induced wind: a) electrode geometry;
 b) electrode polarity; c) voltage, current;
 d) crossflow?

2) What is the effect(s) of corona wind
 on particle motion and when it is
 comparable to coulombic drift?

3) Can corona wind particle
 transport be used to
 improve ESP design?

A numerical model and experimental
 measurement of corona wind and its
 effect on particle motion

METHODS

Data

1) Numerical model
 -gas velocity, dispersion
  coefficient
 -particle velocity, particle size
 -electric field, charge
  distribution

2) Experimental
 -gas velocity, turbulence
  intensity
 -particle velocity, size
 -current, voltage

Analysis

 -statistical analyses to yield turbulence
  intensity and turbulent dispersion data
 -comparison between numerical and experimental
  results
 -development of scaling laws for corona wind
 -comparison of convective and turbulent particle
  transport velocities with coulombic drift
  velocity
 -sensitivity, error analysis

Knowledge Claim (hypothesis)

Corona wind is an important particle transport
mechanism in ESPs.

Value Claim (hypothesis)

Present design of ESPs could be
modified to take advantage of
corona wind.

FIGURE 3-4 Work-plan outline—mechanical/electrical engineering.

FIGURE 3-5 Work-plan outline—resource planning.

THEORY

The structure of our government is not that of a pure democracy, but that of a republic

There have been a number of participation crises in U.S. history where citizens have attempted to make the government more democratic, and we are in the middle of another.

The major focus during the current crisis is on the bureaucracy.

There have been enormous pressures to increase public participation in Forest Service decision making.

Today the Forest Service recognizes the legitimacy of public participation, and is committed to seeking out the public's view.

Concepts: democracy
             republic
             bureaucracy
             public
             public participation
             Forest Service
             national forest planning

Problem:

There is a scarcity of social science research analyzing who participates, how they are involved, why they become involved, and which methods for involving the public in resource decisionmaking should be used.

Public Participation in National Forest Planning

1. Who participates in formal public involvement opportunities?

2. Why are some participants less active than others?

3. What methods do participants must frequently use to get involved?

4. Do participants have preferences for certain methods?

5. What motivates people to participate?

6. Do differences in motivation exist among participants?

If motivational groups are identified:

7. Do these groups prefer certain methods?

"The war is not over." Public participation is likely to increase in the future, and both the public and the Forest Service have a long way to go in dealing with each other. This study can be part of a long-term education process for both groups.

METHODS

Data
    Results from a 12-page mail questionnaire

Analysis
    Data will be analyzed using the Statistical Package for Social Sciences (SPSSX). Because of the nature of the data, primarily non-parametric statistics will be used.

Knowledge claims

Public participation is skewed in the direction of upper-status citizens.

Inactive participants represent themselves on most occasions.

Active participants represent an organization on most occasions.

Value claims:

Results of this study will add to our understanding of the participants themselves and which methods for involving the public should be used. Participant preferences for certain methods could become an asset to managers in guaranteeing a larger and more interested public.

examination or the final thesis defense. If, from the beginning, you conceive of your research as a combination of concepts and methods, you will have a realistic notion of what research is all about. By attempting a V in the early stages of your project, and coming back to it periodically as your research progresses—as your ideas become more sophisticated and clear—working to change and improve the V can focus your efforts toward development of a more balanced set of research skills.

Chapter 4

Grant Proposals

Chapter 3 discussed writing a work plan for your research project. With a little reemphasis and elaboration, this work plan can be tailored to the specifications of a particular funding agency and submitted as a grant proposal—a request for money to support all or part of your research. Sometimes work plans are developed as grant proposals from the start, either because this is the institution's required format or because there is a genuine need for additional research funds. However, it may help you to know that there is *not* a clear and direct relationship between the amount of financial support received and the quality of the research done. Although there is certainly a lower limit below which you cannot carry out your project (some areas of research require, for example, expensive equipment), low-budget research can be, and often is, some of the best.

Big budgets can even have negative effects on research.[23] Abundant funding can reduce your focus on the actual research and turn your attention unproductively to management of equipment and people and development of overly complicated methods. You may feel obliged to conduct your study in complex ways that may lead to reams of computer output but little real insight. If a limited budget forces you to streamline your work and to focus on achieving your objectives in the most efficient manner, it can be a significant benefit to your first research project.

Nevertheless, while it would be nice to simply work up a project and then go ahead and carry it out, this is often not possible without some outside support. *Grantsmanship* is the art of getting financial support (a grant) for your research. Without grant-getting skills, it is likely that you will eventually have to settle for doing research originated primarily by others, or doing tasks other than research to provide financial support so that you can do the work you want to do in your extra time.

In attempting to find money to support all or part of your research project, it helps to have some idea of why agencies give grants. An agency or institution is dedicated, usually by established policy, to use its money for certain purposes. To effectively accomplish this mission, it could set up its own facilities, hiring and training its own personnel to do the work, or it could give the money to specialists already trained and equipped to do the work at other agencies or institutions. Agencies that follow the latter course often request proposals so that they can select those that best suit their purposes. (Some agencies, such as the USDA Forest Service, attempt to maximize their productivity by combining these two approaches.) Above all, an agency looks for research that is well assured to result in a product or information that will be of value to the agency within its constraints of money and time.

Obtaining research support should be viewed as a cooperative, symbiotic relationship in which both researcher and agency can do more with the help of the other than either can do alone. The agency provides money; the researcher provides expertise. Above and beyond doing the actual research, you will be obligated to keep the granting agency informed of your progress (through, at minimum, annual progress reports) and your results (through a carefully written final report). You should also be prepared to spend time with representatives from the granting agency when they visit your institution and to set up show-and-tell sessions demonstrating progress in your work. You are also expected to acknowledge, in a fairly conspicuous way, the agency's support when you publish or talk about the work.

BASIC VS. APPLIED RESEARCH

Research is commonly characterized, according to its objectives, as either basic (fundamental) or applied (practical). *Basic research* is concerned with the acquisition of facts or with questions of how the universe is constructed and how its various components function, regardless of whether this knowledge can be applied to benefit humans. *Applied research* is concerned only with the application to human affairs of general principles and fundamental facts. In the strictest sense, basic research is without cause. It is carried out for the sake of inquiry only, not because the knowledge is needed. In contrast, applied research is dedicated to a cause. Its primary purpose is utilization of facts.

In practice, drawing a clear line between basic and applied research is difficult and, in most cases, not desirable. Ultimately, even the most basic research results have applications that can benefit humanity. In the short term, whether your own research is deemed basic or applied depends, to a rather large extent, on how *you* view it. To obtain support, it matters perhaps even more how you present your research to others. Most agencies and institutions traditionally support only certain types of research. For example, the National Science Foundation (NSF) and many private research foundations have a strong history of support for basic research. Other agencies, such as the USDA, support more applied research. Within a university, some departments, such as botany, zoology, chemistry, or physics, favor basic research. Other departments, such as entomology, forestry, or engineering, favor applied research. Within these departments, individual professors have preferences for different types of research.

The current trend, however, is toward more applied research. As money for research has become less readily available, researchers are being called upon more often to justify their work in terms of human benefit. Most research projects can be presented from either a basic or an applied perspective. One of the necessary survival skills you must learn is to identify potential benefits to others of the work you want to do. Sometimes this connection is tenuous, but for the large majority of research, a convincing case can be built for the ultimate utility of the work.

SOURCES OF FUNDING

The main people to start checking for potential sources of funding are your advisor, other professors, and the college and university grants and contracts officers. The university grants office may publish a monthly newsletter listing current funding opportunities. When an agency wishes to solicit proposals, it may distribute a formal request for proposals, or RFP. RFPs are often sent to university grant offices and to professors and other researchers in the general specialty area. You may also write or phone an agency to describe your ideas for a research project and ask if there is any possibility of support for such a project.

Regardless of whether a formal RFP is available, here is the information that you will need to get from the funding agency before preparing and submitting a proposal:

1 *Topic or subject area to be funded:* If your project does not fit into this subject area, it is a waste of time to submit a proposal.

2 *Amount and duration of funding:* There may be a maximum amount the agency will give for a single proposal. Time restrictions vary. One year is perhaps most common. NSF grants are usually for 3 years.

3 *Restrictions as to who can apply:* Some funding, for example, is available only to first-year graduate students, to people no more than 5 years past their Ph.D., to university faculty, or to people of a certain sex or affiliation.

4 *Deadline:* If there is a stated deadline, pay close attention to it so that you can get your proposal in on time. After writing the proposal, time (up to a week or more) must be allowed to obtain official approval signatures on the proposal and, possibly, for getting the proposal to the agency. Check whether the proposal must be only *postmarked* by the deadline or actually *at* the agency by that date. In the latter case, you will need to mail your proposal

1 week or more in advance to ensure that it will arrive in time. If you are pressed for time, invest in one of the overnight, guaranteed-delivery mailing systems. However, don't put excess faith in these; they are far from as infallible as their advertising suggests. If you only need to get your proposal postmarked by the deadline, life is somewhat simpler. The best approach, of course, is to finish the proposal far in advance, but, in reality, researchers sometimes arrive at the post office at 4:59 P.M. on the deadline date. There are also grim stories of packages that got put aside at the post office and not postmarked till the next day and, hence, were not even considered for funding. Though only a few agencies are completely rigid about deadlines, the deadline should always be taken seriously.

5 *Format:* Guidelines for proposal writing vary from very general to very specific, but some guidelines are usually provided. The agency might specify a page limit (such as 3 or 16 pages maximum) and details of budget presentation and main topic headings. These guidelines are usually some variation of what is presented under the "guidelines" section on p. 74.

6 *Number of copies:* An agency may request up to 30 copies of your proposal. Get the title page signed before making copies so that each copy has all the official signatures. Send along the original signature page only if it is specifically requested.

7 *Where to send:* If you are asked to send the proposal to a general agency address, call and find out who will deal directly with the subject matter of your proposal, and send an extra copy of the proposal directly to that person, with a brief cover letter. Make it clear, however, that you have sent the appropriate number of copies to the general address.

AIM AND STRUCTURE OF A GRANT PROPOSAL

A research proposal has three important aims. First, it must justify the need for the particular research. It must convince others that a problem exists and that something should be done about it. The proposal must clearly show that the work to date in this area is inadequate—incomplete, poorly done, or not done—and that further research is necessary.

Second, a proposal must show that you are qualified and equipped to do the work. In your proposal, you must demonstrate that you have the background to undertake the project and that you know how you will manage such things as personnel, funds, and time. Include a detailed timetable and a description of available resources, both human and material, necessary for the research. Once you have actually done the research, it is not usually appropriate to outline all the logistics of how it was done, but since you have not yet done the research, such detail is the only way that the reviewer can determine whether you really know what you will do and how good your chances are of achieving your objectives. .

Last, the proposal must demonstrate that no matter what results you get, you will produce information useful to the funding agency. You must make it clear that the work proposed is realistic and that it will have value regardless of whether your hypothesis is correct. You might provide a series of working hypotheses, any of which, true or not, will provide useful information. Include when possible, a description of pertinent preliminary experiments.

Anything that helps make these points clear to the reviewer can be used. Diagrams or illustrations can be included just about anywhere. Similarly, a table of contents and extensive use of headings and subheadings will help the reviewer more easily find pertinent sections of a lengthy proposal.

The structure of a research proposal reflects these considerations. Because the aim of the proposal is to convince others that the work should be done and that you can do it, the introduction gets straight to the point by first succinctly stating the problem and the research objectives. This is then backed up by a justification statement and a description of the current state of knowledge in the area. Direct users of research results are described, and projections made on how the results will be used. In the methods section, choice of methods is justified whenever possible. Methods are followed by a detailed timetable, a listing of personnel and cooperators and their roles, an itemization of your facilities and institutional experience, and a budget. These items constitute a management plan for the research. They emphasize your commitment to the work and show that you will do it in a certain way on a specific schedule. They convince the reviewer that the work you propose to do is realistic.

According to a National Institutes of Health study,[11] the most frequently cited reasons for rejection of a proposal were: questionable project design (overly ambitious or unrealistic, vague purpose, questionable procedures, unimportant problem); inadequate explanation (the proposal was too vague and lacked detail); and questionable competence of the investigator (inadequate experience, lack of understanding of the literature, insufficient liaison with colleagues in the field).

PEOPLE AND PROPOSALS

Because research, especially externally supported research, is a cooperative enterprise, the "people" aspects of your project are very important. Without a demonstrably strong network of human support, even an excellent proposal from an unknown researcher does not have a very good chance of being funded. As a graduate student, you are probably an unknown in research circles and have no established track record in this endeavor, so you must build up a convincing support network in your proposal. This gives the proposal weight and substance that it would not otherwise have. For example, putting an established researcher (your advisor or another faculty member) on as coprincipal investigator (co-PI) will add the weight of his or her professional reputation. In some institutions and with some advisors, the student is not even allowed to *be* a principal investigator (PI) for this reason. The student writes the proposal, with the professor's help. The professor submits it under his or her name, and the student does the work. This approach may get you the funds but, unless you are listed as a principal investigator, you will not get credit for getting the grant and cannot add it to your record. And a Catch-22 of research is that you can't get grants without having a record of getting grants. An alternative approach (if you have a strong commitment to future research) is to submit a very modest proposal under your own name—a proposal that seems well-assured of success and that will not cost the granting agency much. Grants specifically for graduate research projects are available from NSF and other agencies. Once you have shown a funding agency that you can do well, you have begun to build the appropriate track record for obtaining future, and larger, research grants.

Include a strong "cooperation" section in your proposal, and be sure to contact directly each of the people and agencies from whom you will be expecting cooperation during the project. Obtain their verbal or written support for the project before listing them. You can lose a great deal of credibility if a cooperator finds out about his or her expected participation secondhand.

To add further clout to your proposal, you can solicit letters of support for your project from well-known people in the research area. Send them a copy of the proposal for review, and ask for a letter of support to attach to it (in an appendix). Conversely, avoid including anything in your proposal that might suggest that you personally might not know enough to handle the work. For example, play down your student status whenever possible and don't mention coursework. Call your written report a final report, not a thesis.

GENERAL GUIDELINES FOR PROPOSAL PREPARATION

Proposals submitted for review prior to preparation of the final copy should be double-spaced to allow room for reviewers' comments. The final copy sent to the agency can be single-spaced unless the agency specifies otherwise. The final copy must be letter-quality—that is, it must look as if it had been typed with a carbon ribbon. (Some high-quality dot matrix printers can produce this effect.) Good photocopies are acceptable. The original (except, sometimes, the original signature page) does not need to be sent.

The following are guidelines to the format and contents of a typical grant proposal:

1   Title Page
Brief descriptive title
Principal investigator(s) and signature(s)
Institutional address and telephone number
Amount requested

Desired starting date and probable duration of project
Approval signatures (for example, department chairperson, college dean, university financial officer)

2 Abstract The abstract goes on a separate page following the title page. It should be no longer than one paragraph, and should include brief, clear statements of the need for the work, the research objectives, the approach to be used, and the anticipated results and their significance. A poor abstract is one that focuses heavily on methods. (In preparing the proposal, it may be easiest to write the abstract last, even though it appears first in the final document.)

Because the abstract precedes the proposal itself, and because reviewers like a bit of orientation, the abstract is nearly always the first part of the proposal read during the review process. It must be written clearly and simply. If you cannot attract the interest of the reviewer in your abstract, your cause may be lost.[8]

3 Problem Statement and Objectives Clearly state the intent for which the project is being undertaken and include a justification. Phrase your justification in terms of human need and/or specific gaps in knowledge that the work is intended to fill. References are important but they must be pertinent. Specifics are reserved for the next section. Provide a clear statement of objectives. Take great care in selecting words and phrases for your objectives. If the proposal is funded, any subsequent report or evaluation will be focused on these statements. For your own sake, emphasize low-risk objectives.

Some agencies require a "justification" section separate from the problem statement. Because it is difficult to separate these two items, you may find that you are repeating yourself. A certain amount of redundancy is, fortunately, appropriate in a proposal because each reviewer will probably not read all sections with equal interest.

4 State of Knowledge Give detailed background information leading up to the present status of the problem. (In a thesis, this section is usually called "literature review" or "background.")

5 Methods Include a step-by-step description of all procedures necessary for study completion. Methods should follow the stated objectives in a clear and logical manner. All phases of the study must be covered, including, for example, site selection, experimental and sampling design, measurement techniques, data management, and analysis procedures. Whenever possible, provide a rationale or justification for the methods chosen. Show that you have considered alternative methods. If pilot tests or preliminary experiments are to be done, describe them. If preliminary experiments have already been done and your results can be used to strengthen the case for the rest of the work, bring this up in your introductory sections, not here.

6 Timetable Make this detailed and be sure to include time for preparation of a final report prior to completion of the project.

7 Personnel Provide the names and titles of the main people on the project—principal investigator(s) and any others (such as technicians or temporary help) listed in the budget. Briefly describe areas of responsibility for each. Make it clear that both PIs, if there are two, will play an important role in the project, that neither is only a figurehead. For each PI, refer to a vitae in the proposal appendix.

8 Cooperation Your project will require the resources of other individuals (such as those with special methodological skills) or agencies (to provide materials or access to a laboratory or a field site). List all these human resources that will help you with this project but that are not included in the budget. Tell what each will do.

9 Capability Statement (or Facilities) Include a description of all institutional nonhuman resources that are available and necessary for your work. Show that you are equipped to do the work and have the right sort of laboratory setups or field sites or both. For example:[12]

> The facilities at ———University are well suited to all phases of the proposed research. Our laser laboratory is equipped with a variety of

lasers including a 1-MW nitrogen laser and two pulsed tunable dye lasers. This laboratory is also equipped with an optical table, and an array of polarizing optics and photodetectors. Signal processing equipment includes a PET minicomputer interfaced to a terminal, an x-y recorder, and two stepping motors and detectors. Specialized mounts can be fabricated in the university's machine shop. We also have about 200 square feet of preparative laboratory space, equipped with ample glassware and equipment for sample preparation. Departmental facilities which will be available to this program include two Perkin-Elmer fluorescence spectrometers (MPF-2A), two Spex double monochromators, and a Cary 14 absorption spectrometer. . . .

10   Budget   As soon as you start working out research costs, you will realize that these costs are not rigid or even particularly objective. You could do your research very cheaply by, for example, camping out and cooking for yourself and doing all the work yourself instead of hiring assistants. However, submitting a "bare-bones" budget is undesirable for many reasons. Your first concern should be for optimizing the research itself. Doing your research well should have higher priority than saving money. If eating at restaurants would save you energy and time during a field study, for example, and would permit you to focus on your rescarch more efficiently, you should consider asking for funds to do this. Similarly, if having a helper in the laboratory or field would facilitate your doing the research rapidly and effectively, consider asking for money to cover this.

Start working out a budget by listing all the things in your project for which you could use funding. Then make appropriate compromises between optimizing your research and the financial constraints dictated by the agency. If your total is too high (and it probably will be), start pruning it down, but don't submit a budget that risks being too low. There are always unexpected expenses, so a little leeway is needed. In any case, your budget should be realistic, and what is realistic will seem high to you when you start doing research.

It will save you some worry to know that the level of funding initially requested is usually *not* a deciding factor in whether your proposal is successful. In the National Institutes of Health study[11] discussed earlier, budgets were seldom considered a problem and were even more rarely grounds for rejection. Your budget is a problem only if it is absurdly high or if you refuse to negotiate and alter it (usually down but sometimes up) as suggested by the agency. Proposal reviewers are often specifically asked to evaluate only the basic quality of the proposal and its relevance to the goals of the agency. *Then* the budget is evaluated and negotiated. If the agency likes your proposal but feels that the budget is too high (that is, they think you could do it more cheaply, or they can't afford it), they will give you a chance to modify it. For example, they might like your proposal but can provide only $10,000 of the $16,000 you requested. Then it is up to you to figure out what parts of the research you will have to cut out and what you will keep to do it for that amount.

In working up this budget, keep in mind that all figures are only estimates at this point in the work. While you cannot expect to get more money if you run out during the research, you can usually move money from one category to another (for example, from temporary help to supplies) if necessary. Equipment and travel funds are usually scrutinized more closely by funding agencies than are other categories. Expect to either forgo some of these items or to be able to strongly justify their inclusion and to negotiate them with the agency.

Budget Format   (Figure 4-1) If you are asking for funding for less than 2 years, you can probably get away with lumping all costs into two columns—costs covered by the university and those requested from the agency. For longer time periods, it is helpful and sometimes required to break down costs by year and then have a total column for both university and agency. Budget estimates should be detailed with regard to:

(a)   *Salaries and wages* of all people at your institution who will be involved in the work. List PIs by name. Give percent involvement for PIs and estimated work time and hourly wages of temporary help. A graduate assistantship, which is what you are probably seeking, is considered a half-time appointment. The salary is predetermined by your department, college, or institution, for 9-month (academic year) or 12-month (annual) assistantships. While teaching assistantships are generally 9-month, research assistantships are usually 12-month and include the summer

BUDGET ESTIMATES

	Year 1		Year 2		Total	
	[Institution]	[Agency]	[Institution]	[Agency]	[Institution]	[Agency]
1) Salaries and Wages						
Principal investigators						
[faculty member], 5%	$1,000	–	$1,080	–	$2,080	–
[student], 50%	–	6,610	–	7,140	–	13,750
Temporary help, 1						
summer month	–	900	–	972	–	1,872
Fringe benefits						
23% senior personnel	230	–	248	–	478	–
10% other	–	751	–	811	–	1,562
Total salaries and wages	1,230	8,261	1,328	8,923	2,558	17,184
2) Supplies						
Seedling containers, fertilizer, petri dishes	–	200	–	140	–	340
Chemical for trace mineral analysis	–	–	–	669	–	660
3) Equipment						
1 power supply (Heathkit SP-2717)	–	275	–	–	–	275
4) Travel						
Field work (per diem and vehicle costs)	–	800	–	650	–	1,450
National meeting SAF (date, location)	–	–	–	800	–	800
5) Miscellaneous Costs						
Phone, computer, copying, postage, secretarial	100	300	200	300	300	600
Publication	–	–	–	600	–	600
6) Total Direct Costs	1,330	9,836	1,528	12,073	2,858	21,909
7) Indirect Costs						
(30% total direct costs minus equipment)	339	2,868	428	3,622	857	6,490
TOTAL ESTIMATED COSTS	$1,729	$12,704	$1,986	$15,695	$3,715	$28,399

Total requested from [agency] is $28,399. Total contribution from [Institution] is $3,715 or 8.8% of total costs.

FIGURE 4-1 Sample budget page.

months. You will probably want to request a 12-month assistantship. Or you could request a half-time, 9-month appointment, plus full-time pay for 2 to 3 summer months.

If your budget is broken down by year, include a substantial raise for all personnel each year. Ten percent is a reasonable figure. If you don't do this, the institution will go ahead and routinely give people raises and this will have to be taken out of other parts of your budget.

(b) *Fringe benefits* are added to salary, at a rate determined by your institution, to cover insurance, sick leave, and so on. Specify rates used to compute these benefits. Since these rates can change as often as every 6 months, check with the campus grants office for the most recent figures.

(c) *Supplies* usually include expendable or low-cost items such as glassware, thermometers, and so on.

(d) *Equipment:* List here the more expensive and permanent items you will need, such as power supplies, microscopes, refrigerators, freezers, and so on. Many smaller items that you might consider equipment would best be listed as supplies

There is a trade-off in asking for large equipment items in a research proposal. On one hand, you would like the agency to know that you have all the equipment needed to carry out the proposed research. On the other hand, you may really be missing one or two critical items. If you do ask for equipment, add a justification for these items following the budget or as an appendix to the proposal. Some agencies specifically request a justification statement for equipment items costing more than, say, $300 each.

(e) *Travel:* Include first any costs for travel necessary to do the actual research. For ground transport, give mileage rates, daily vehicle costs, and estimated total mileage upon which your estimate is based. Then add lodging and food costs (per diem) for people doing the travel. Find out your university's limits and rules on this. For example, you might be allowed actual costs (verified by saved receipts) of whatever lodging you can find (say, $30 per night for a motel room) plus either actual food costs (again, save receipts) or a fixed amount (such as $20 per day) for food.

It is important that you present your research at a professional meeting of some type. If this sort of travel is not specifically proscribed in the RFP, ask for money to cover it. Include air fare or vehicle costs, plus per diem and registration fees, and specify the date and title of the meeting. This item may eventually get negotiated out of your grant, but it's still worth a try.

(f) *Miscellaneous* expenses might include phone, photocopying, mailing, secretarial assistance, computer costs, and publication. List computer costs in a separate category if they are high—greater than $500, for example. Publication of a single research paper in a reviewed and prestigious journal in some areas (such as the biological sciences) may cost $50 to $100 per page.

A minimum of one publication every 2 years is expected on a

project. Because the time period of the grant may run out before your article is accepted for publication and actual page and reprint costs determined, some way of handling the money allocated for publication may have to be worked out with your institution ahead of time.

(g)   *Overhead* (indirect costs): These are costs you must usually tack onto your budget to help the university cover such things as building upkeep and administrative services. While these are necessary costs and considerations, it can be discouraging at first to realize that, if you get the grant, you get only the total amount *minus* the overhead and fringe-benefit costs to actually use for your research. Thus you will have to ask the agency for considerably more money than you personally need to do the research. Fortunately, this is standard practice and expected by funding agencies. Overhead rates are established in different ways at each institution and vary enormously—from 20 to 100 percent of total costs. Some independent consulting agencies with good reputations charge 200 percent overhead. Overhead can be based on a percent of the total budget (usually minus equipment costs) or on salaries and wages only. Find out the current rate at your institution and specify it in your budget.

Matching Costs or Cost-Sharing   Agencies often like to see that your institution is supporting your research to some extent, that you have institutional backing of a concrete sort. Some agencies require a minimum match, or sharing of costs (say, 5 percent). This means that you must show how your university will pay for at least that percent of the costs of the work. There are several ways to generate matching money in the university column of the budget:

(a)   Talk with your advisor, the department chairperson, or the college financial officer, and get the university to provide some vehicle costs, secretarial help, computer costs, or some other part of the actual expenses of the work.

(b)   Include your advisor or another faculty member as co-PI for an appropriate percentage of his or her time (say, 3 to 5 percent), and add that percentage of his or her salary to the university column as matching costs.

(c)   See if your budget administrators will allow you to ask for less overhead from the agency. If they do, put the remaining portion of the overhead costs in the university column.

If a matching requirement is not stated in the RFP, it is important to check into this. While a few agencies would prefer that you not include any cost-sharing, others might expect you to know that they have a minimum cost-sharing rate. In general, the more cost-sharing you show, the happier it makes the funding agency. If you are already supported to some extent by your institution (on an assistantship, for example) and are asking for only a portion of the research costs, show this clearly.

At the bottom of the budget, specify exactly how much you are requesting from the agency and how much you are matching, in dollars and percents.

11   Literature Cited

12   Appendices   Include vitae of principal investigator(s), examples of relevant work, letters of support, details of methodology—anything that adds to the proposal but that would interrupt the reviewer's flow of thought or would make the body of the proposal overlong and boring if included there.

A *curriculum vitae* is an academic term for what the rest of the world calls a résumé. In it, include your name, address, phone number, education, experience, society membership and service, awards, and publications as appropriate. If you have no awards, omit an awards section. If you have no publications, but have attended meetings and given some talks, you might replace the publications section with "Meetings and Presentations."

The aim of any vitae or résumé is to demonstrate that you are highly qualified for a particular job, promotion, or grant. Every time you use a vitae, it should be revised with a particular goal in mind. Prepare the proposal vitae to emphasize your qualifications to do the proposed research. You want the granting agency to get the idea that you will do little except work at your research. Mentioning that you have three toddlers will not help your case. Listing several hobbies is also not appropriate. Omit other extraneous information such as height, weight, birth date, health, marital status, and references. In any vitae that you send out, include such personal information only if it is directly relevant to your objective. If your research includes a lot of heavy field work, it might not hurt to mention that you are in good physical condition and lift weights as a hobby. Similarly, a field research project might make it appropriate to mention that you like to backpack.

SUBMITTING THE PROPOSAL

When the proposal is finished and you have done the best you can at the time, you will probably still feel uncomfortable about some aspects of it—perhaps lack of clarity in describing your methods or not aiming it exactly at the needs of the agency. However, once it is submitted, the quality of the proposal as you perceive it is only one of many factors that affect whether it will be funded. Overriding factors are available money, who reviews the proposal, and any one of a dozen other things. You can spend 3 months working up what you believe is a superb proposal, one that couldn't possibly be beaten for quality, and not get funded. Or you might get an RFP late or hear, via the grapevine, of some available money, then spend an afternoon whipping up a proposal to meet a deadline and get $50,000 for your efforts. So there is no need to anguish over what *you* perceive of as deficiencies in your proposal, once it is submitted.

TIMING

After the grant is submitted, several months may pass before you learn whether you will get any funding. Even after a dollar figure is agreed upon, it may be several more months before you can actually spend any of the grant money. This delay will be less frustrating if you expect it. Though it may be difficult to start the project without the grant, do what you can. If the project is partly done by the time you receive the money and get an official starting date, this is to your benefit. It ensures that you will be done by the official ending date (which is usually 1, 2, or 3 years from the date that the funds are officially okayed) and that you will be able to turn in a good final report on time. "Bootlegging" research on a shoestring or on other funds until grant funds are obtained is standard practice among many productive researchers. The agency gets results fast, which pleases them and enhances the researcher's reputation. Then the researcher can spend some of the funds getting a jump on the *next* research project.

Chapter 5

Thinking in Research

Recall that scientific research is the testing of ideas (in the form of hypotheses). Research involves a way in which ideas are generated and then a way in which they are treated. From this perspective, research can be regarded as consisting of two interacting sets of processes that go on at the same time—imaginative processes and critical processes. These are very different from each other but are equally important in research. The aim of the imaginative steps is discovery, the generation of new ideas by intuition. The aim of the critical steps is verification or falsification of ideas. In research, you can't proceed to the testing phase until you have ideas for hypotheses to test, and the tests, in turn, produce new ideas for hypotheses to test.

Because ideas are so important in research, it can help to know something about them. Ideas are not derived exclusively, or even mainly, from conscious thought (reasoning). If this is so, where do they come from? To start, let's look at Dewey's[9] analysis of the thinking process. First we become aware of a problem and

Imaginative ◄——————► Critical

Aim: Discovery   Validation/Falsification

Key Mental
    Process: Intuition   Reason or logic

FIGURE 5-1   Mental processes used in research.

this awareness provides a stimulus toward a solution. In research, this first step is something we do at the conscious level. We study the problem and work on it. Some time after we have become aware of a problem and have developed a desire to solve it, a possible solution may spring into the conscious mind. This step is largely out of our control. Conjuring up an idea or possible solution to a problem is not a deliberate, voluntary act. It is something that happens to us, rather than something we do. However, once we have the idea, reason (logical thought) can come back into play to examine the idea.

INTUITION

The creative process—the generation of new ideas—is called intuition. An idea generated by intuition is sometimes called a hunch, an insight, an illumination, or, on a grander scale, an inspiration or revelation. More formally, an intuition is a sudden enlightenment or comprehension of a situation, a clarifying idea that springs into the consciousness, often when one is not consciously thinking about the subject.[2] The most characteristic circumstances of an intuition are a period of intense work on a problem, accompanied by a strong desire for its solution, then temporary abandonment of the work, perhaps with attention to something else, then the appearance of the idea (or intuition) with dramatic suddenness. There is often a sense of certainty, and a feeling of exhilaration and perhaps surprise that the idea had not been thought of before.

There are many, many examples, in all fields of science, of important intuitions. Most of our greatest discoveries have, at their center, a key intuition that occurred, all of a sudden, when the discoverer's mind was not focused on the particular problem. A classic and oft-quoted example is that of the German chemist Kekulé who went to bed after a bout of drinking and dreamed of six monkeys chasing one another in a circle, the tail of one held in the teeth of the other. This dream gave the scientist the clue to the structure of benzene and of cyclic carbon compounds.

Regardless of the scale, most of your ideas originate in a similar manner and, though you cannot force yourself to have an idea, there are ways to facilitate having them. First, you need a strong desire for a solution. Prepare your mind. Develop a dissatisfaction with your understanding of a situation, a dissatisfaction that gives you a need to know the answer. As Pasteur said, "Chance favors the prepared mind." That is, the variety and quality of ideas that occur to you are, to a great extent, functions of how well prepared your mind is by past experience and education pertinent to the particular problem. And you do have some control over the sorts of experiences and educational activities to which you are exposed. Setting your mind to work on a research problem then involves preparation of both a general nature (education, experience) and of a specific nature (working on your particular problem to generate within yourself the desire for further understanding).

But once you have done all of this, once you are as aware of the problem and of the need for a solution as you can be at that particular time, get away from the problem for a while. If you keep focusing on your problem beyond a certain point, you interfere with the creative process. Stop thinking directly about the problem. Do something that relaxes your mind and allows it to work by itself on the problem. Go for a walk, for example, or work on some of the more mechanical aspects of the research, like tabulating data or cleaning up the lab.

This technique is extremely helpful for generating ideas because your subconscious mind continues to work on a problem when you have stopped consciously thinking about it. It is essential to leave time for this subconscious assimilation of information. Maxwell Maltz[19] said that:

[A]fter [the researcher] has defined the problem, sees in his imagination the desired end result, secured all the information and facts that he can, then additional struggling, fretting and worrying over it do not help, but seem to hinder the solution.

It is useful to think of your subconscious mind as a goal-seeking mechanism, like a guided missile. In research, your subconscious mind acts as an automatic creative mechanism—a source of new ideas—relevant to solving your research problem. Once you consciously program your mind to seek a particular goal (that is, work on a problem and want an answer), your mind will continue to seek a solution even when you are not aware of it. A similar thing happens when you are, for example, hungry. Your subconscious mind is programmed to seek food and, when you are hungry, regardless of how hard you try to ignore the rumbling of your empty stomach, thoughts of food and of places to get it will continually pop into your conscious mind.

If you really mean business, have an intense desire [to solve the problem], and begin to think intensely about all angles of the problem—your creative mechanism [your subconscious mind] goes to work—and [scans] through stored information [and works toward] an answer. It selects an idea here, a fact there, a series of former experiences, and relates them—or "ties them together" into a meaningful whole which will "fill out" the incompleted portion of your situation, complete your equation, or "solve" your problem. When this solution is served up to your consciousness [your conscious mind]—often at an unguarded moment when you are thinking of something else—or perhaps even as a dream while your consciousness is asleep—something "clicks" and you at once "recognize" this as the answer you have been searching for.[19]

Bertrand Russell, one of our greatest thinkers, said:

I have found . . . that, if I have to write upon some rather difficult topic, . . . the best plan is to think about it with very great intensity—the greatest intensity of which I am capable—for a few hours or days, and at the end of that time give orders, so to speak, that the work is to proceed underground. After some months I return consciously to the topic and find that the work has been done. Before I had discovered this technique, I used to spend the intervening months worrying because I was making no progress; I arrived at the solution none the sooner for this worry, and the intervening months were wasted, whereas now I can devote them to other pursuits.[24]

In practical terms, this tells us several things. One is that all work and no play not only make Jack a dull boy but a poor researcher as well. A certain periodicity, an alternation of days or hours of hard, conscious labor on a research problem, with time to relax and think and, consciously at least, get away from the problem, is perhaps the best recipe for quality research. Many good researchers and productive thinkers, for example, spend their last few minutes in the office or laboratory at the end of the day concentrating upon a particularly important problem, focusing and programming their mind to work on it subconsciously until they return to work on it consciously the next day. They "sleep on it."

While many researchers do their best work during long periods of uninterrupted mental concentration, some find they gain much more productivity by working on the intellectual aspects of a problem intensely for an hour or two at a time rather than working continuously. For nearly all researchers, however, long periods of uninterrupted time to devote to a *combination* of the intellectual and mechanical aspects of research are essential.

Because the mental processes necessary for discovery in research are a function of your subconscious mind and cannot be turned off and on at will, successful research cannot be done on a strict 9 A.M. to 5 P.M. basis. Nor is research something that can be squeezed into an hour or two of spare time during a day filled with other tasks, especially if the other tasks require a lot of thought or attention. Because it is carried out independently and depends to a large extent upon the researcher's inner drive or motivation, research usually progresses in a somewhat irregular manner. Only occasionally is a researcher hotly pursuing a new discovery. At such times, you need to pour all your energies into the work and think of it day and night. Unfortunately, such spurts of activity are all too rare, so it is important to be ready to take advantage of them when they do occur. On the other hand, freshness and originality may be lost when you work unceasingly for too long.

The other side of the coin is, of course, procrastination. The prospect of having to grapple with a knotty problem or, later on, to write major sections of your thesis, tends to bring on a flurry of displacement activities. This is not necessarily a bad thing. Contemplating a difficult job is often the only way my desk gets cleaned up properly. Eventually, however, a sense of urgency about the task develops as time runs short and the deadline comes closer. Setting a series of deadlines for yourself when you plan your research can be very helpful in this respect.

Nevertheless, once you get going on your research, keep at it. Work on your project nearly every day for at least an hour. Persistence is more important than native intelligence. There are many extremely intelligent people who lack the persistence necessary to carry a project through difficult spots. When you come to a difficult part, don't kid yourself into believing that you are analyzing your approach or reviewing your work when you are actually avoiding a decision or just plain loafing. After time away from your research, or a period of work on some of the more mechanical aspects of the research, bring your conscious mind back to the difficulty and at least refresh your understanding of the questions or problems that exist. Keep doing this until a solution presents itself.

Another technique that can help you generate ideas is discussion. In explaining the problem to another person, especially to someone not familiar with that field of science, you must clarify and amplify aspects of it that may have been taken for granted, and the familiar chain of thought is interrupted.[2] Not uncommonly, an idea occurs when you are making the explanation. A new thought may occur without the other person having said a word. (This is why we often say that you really don't understand something until you have tried to teach it.)

The other person in the discussion, by asking questions—even ill-informed ones—may cause you to see a new approach to the problem or the connection between two or more observations or ideas that you had not noticed before, that had perhaps been seen but had not registered mentally. On a more formal level, discussions with your committee and at professional meetings can be a tremendous stimulus to ideas, especially when you are beginning to feel stale and bogged down by your work.

When up against an impasse that periods of temporary abandonment and discussion do not seem to solve, it is sometimes helpful to go back to the beginning and to gather some fresh data or to try a new line of approach. A different approach can often provide the perspective you need to understand what is happening. This is one of the reasons why use of more than one method in a research project is considered desirable.

SKEPTICISM

It is not enough to know how to facilitate the production of ideas. You must also realize that our automatic response to a new idea is often rejection. Then we use our conscious minds to defend that rejection. We have, as human beings, an instinctive mental resistance to the unfamiliar.[18] From a biological perspective, this has considerable survival value. Safety often lies in the familiar. Something new must be approached cautiously as it may represent a danger to us or to our families. This fundamental biological propensity for security and safety explains a great deal of human behavior, including the cyclic nature of progress in science. Resistance to new ideas is an integral part of the history of science.[17] Skepticism is often an automatic reaction to protect ourselves from an idea contrary to our familiar view of the world.

Not only do our instincts make it difficult to deal rationally with new ideas, but so do our education and our cultural setting. As we become trained in an area, we learn not only how work *is* done in that area, but also how it is *not* done. Kuhn[17] said that most research is a "strenuous and devoted attempt to force nature into the conceptual boxes supplied by professional education." We all develop, to a greater or lesser extent, a trained incapacity to view our ideas and our research results in a truly objective manner. We take on a perspective closer and closer to prevailing attitudes in the field, whether applied or basic in orientation. Even our source of research funding, our advisors, and the methods we use can influence our interpretation of research findings and the new ideas they generate. An entomologist, for example, may see an insect from a totally different perspective than a zoologist would. A forester will see trees from a different perspective than a botanist will. Ideas and research evidence that are contrary to these area-specific attitudes are often viewed with suspicion.

Bernard[1] remarked, "It is that which we do know which is the great hindrance to our learning, not that which we do not know." This is why outsiders in an area—people trained in other fields—are often the most successful and innovative researchers. Rather than hindering you, changing fields during the course of your education, or even later, can give you a fresh perspective that may set you ahead of others trained solely in your new field. Thus although it may be important that you've had a long personal history of interest in, for example, natural systems, it is not necessary to have begun looking through a microscope or netting insects at age three. Truly innovative research does not come from intense scrutiny of one's own field. Rather, it tends to be generated by exposing oneself to other people and ideas.[4]

An illuminating and useful corollary to the subject of skepticism is the claim that the impact or significance of a piece of research has little to do with truth or empirical proof and a lot to do with whether people find it "interesting."[6] To qualify as interesting, the research findings have to deny certain assumptions or beliefs held by the audience. If all assumptions are denied, the research will be seen as unbelievable or irrelevant. If no assumptions are denied, the research will be seen as obvious, as replowing old ground, as "ho-hum" research. A study designed simply to reaffirm the assumptions of the audience is not likely to be considered significant. Good research—interesting research—falls somewhere between these two extremes. The results must differ moderately from the audience's assumptions in order to surprise and intrigue, but not so much that they are not believed.

In whatever field you choose to work, make an effort to establish a wide and diverse network of contacts both within and outside your field. Read broadly, across disciplines, as much as possible. In your research, take particular care to view each hypothesis as a set of alternative solutions, not one desirable solution. Developing a lack of skepticism—an open-minded receptivity to new ideas and possible solutions—will greatly enhance your skill as a researcher. If you *are* skeptical, be skeptical of your *own* hypotheses. Be your own best critic. Bernard[1] suggested that once the test has begun, the reseacher should try to forget his hypothesis. People who are too fond of their hypotheses, he said, are not well fitted for making discoveries.

CHANCE

In preparing your mind for ideas and creativity in research, it is also essential to recognize the importance of chance. Probably the majority of scientific discoveries, especially the most important and revolutionary ones, have been come upon unexpectedly, or at least had an element of chance in them.[2] Although it is common knowledge that sometimes chance is a factor in the making of a discovery, the magnitude of its importance is seldom realized and the significance of its role is often not fully appreciated or understood. Entire books have been written about the scientific method, omitting any reference to either chance or intuition.

For the beginning researcher, merely recognizing the importance of chance is of considerable help. Then, with practice, you can train your powers of observation and cultivate an attitude of being constantly on the lookout for the unexpected. Make a habit of examining every clue that chance presents. More specifically, don't automatically assume that unexpected results have occurred because your methods were sloppy. This may be true, but it may not. Blaming faulty technique is an easy and very common way to resist facing the real implications of your results. Realize that one often gets the best insights or ideas from experiments that didn't turn out as expccted. Roger Schank, a pioneer in research on artificial intelligence, has found that learning, or discovery, seems to be organized around failed expectations.[14] The discovery hinges upon something not turning out as you expected it to. The "failure" is the key that will often link two apparently unrelated events together in your mind and suggest a possible solution to the problem.

You may also find that even if your objectives are carefully thought out ahead of time, your thesis will end up emphasizing some objectives more than others, and the importance of your work—your discoveries—will not be spread evenly over your predefined set of objectives. In doing research, there is often no direct correlation between effort expended and the value of your results. You might spend 3 months working day and night on one particular aspect of your project and get results that are not particularly important or valuable. Then one afternoon you might notice something new and in 2 hours discover something that ends up occupying a major portion of your thesis.

THE ROLE OF REASON

I have dwelled at length upon the imaginative processes in research because the role of reason has too often been emphasized at their expense. Only the technical parts of research, the testing stages, are even partly objective or rational. In doing research, an overemphasis on the critical processes may actually limit discovery. Important discoveries can be made by paying attention to the points that don't fit the curve, from intense observation of the few data points that don't fit your expectations. The general strategy of research, then, is to work with some clear goal in mind but to keep alert for unexpected opportunities and to take advantage of them.[2]

Let's now consider the relationship between the critical and the imaginative processes, the relationship between discovery and testing, intuition and reason. Logic, or reason, which concerns correctness and validity, has nothing to do with productive thinking. Similarly, intuition, the basis of the production of ideas, is not concerned with correctness and validity. In research, discovery requires an attitude of mind that is different from that required for testing; discovery and testing are distinct processes, each needing a different repertoire of mental skills. A researcher must develop different sets of mental attitudes and skills to use at appropriate times during research. That aspect of a scientist's mind that demands convincing evidence should be reserved for the testing stage of the investigation. Beveridge[2] said:

> The methods and functions of discovery and proof in research are as different as are those of a detective and of a judge in a court of law. While playing the part of the detective, the investigator follows

clues, but having captured his alleged fact, he turns judge and examines the case by means of logically arranged evidence. Both functions are equally essential but they are different.

What, then, is the role of reason? Although discoveries come most often from unexpected results or observations or from intuitions, reason is the principal mental tool in most other aspects of research. Reason is the main tool in formulating hypotheses, in judging the correctness of ideas derived from intuition, in planning experiments, in assessing evidence, and in finding extensions and applications of a new idea or discovery. Like crude ore from a mine, the original discovery is often of little value until it has been refined and fully developed. The role of reason in research is not so much in exploring the frontiers of knowledge as in developing the findings of explorers.[2]

Most people find that they are somewhat better at either imaginative, creative activities or at more logical, critical activities. One of the things that you will learn about yourself in your first research project is where your talents lie. Such knowledge can be used to your advantage in choosing later research projects or areas of study.

Chapter 6

Talking about Research

In addition to acquiring technical proficiency in research, you must be able to communicate—both in writing and in words— what you are doing, and why and how you are doing it. The only way to overcome your nervousness in speaking before a group is through practice, so you might as well start now. You should be able to give a good talk about your research anytime after your work plan has been developed. The only major difference between a talk about incomplete research versus completed research is that, in the former, you describe hypothetical, not actual, results. Talking about research in progress often provides you with feedback from the audience on the strengths and weaknesses of the work, as well as new ideas, which can sharpen and improve both the research itself and the final written report.

Many opportunities exist for telling people about your research: seminars, committee meetings, oral examinations, thesis defenses, and professional meetings, both regional and national. Attend as many professional meetings as is practical during your graduate program and give at least one talk about your research. Look regularly in the main society journals in your field for announcements of meetings and "calls for papers." These often show up 6 months or more before the actual meeting and require you to submit a title and, sometimes, an abstract. Even with work still in progress, it is not difficult to think of and submit a title (or even an abstract) about which you can elaborate when the time comes. Let your advisor and others know that you would like to go to meetings. They can pass along information and help you find ways to cover travel expenses. At some schools, special travel grants are available for graduate students to attend meetings. If you are a research assistant on a grant-funded project, ask your supervisor if the budget can support your travel. This approach is especially likely to succeed if you give a talk (present a "paper") on research funded by the grant.

TALKING VS. WRITING

Talking about research is very different from writing about research because the aims of the two types of communication are different. Whether the talk is as short as 5 minutes or as long as an hour, its primary aim is to generate interest and awareness in the listener, not simply to convey information.[3] While a written account can also generate interest, its main function is to be a source of information. Because of this difference in aims, the rules for giving a research talk are very different from those for writing about research. But once you have a basic understanding of the principles involved in giving a talk and using visual aids effectively, you can probably give a research talk that is better than most talks, even those given by important people at national professional meetings. Researchers who give polished, professional talks are those who understand the basic principles of preparing and delivering oral presentations, who practice, practice, practice, and who *continue* to give each talk the attention and preparation it requires.

Poor Talks and Good Talks

To understand how to give a good talk, first search your memory and recall some of the really poor talks you've had to sit through. What made them poor? Here are some common responses to this question: "The talk was boring. My mind kept drifting away because the subject didn't seem interesting. Even the speaker didn't seem interested in the subject." "There was too much detail." "The speaker was unprepared and kept having to go back and fill in information that he'd missed." "The talk was disorganized and hard to follow." "The slides were poor. They were hard to read and their relationship to the talk was not clear." "The speaker ran out of time and had to hurry at the end. Even so, he went overtime and everyone lost interest." "The speaker talked to the slides, not the audience." And so on.

Audiences do not complain about a speaker's message. They complain about behavior that makes the message difficult to receive.[22] These complaints confirm research showing that 70 to 90 percent of the impact we make on a listener comes not from what we say, but how we say it. Expression, voice, choice of words, and organization carry more weight than the ideas themselves.

In contrast, a good talk is:

- Interesting (not boring)
- Not too technical for the audience
- Well organized
- Not too detailed
- Clear (you understood what the point was)
- Within the allotted time limits
- Enhanced by effective use of visual aids

TWO IMPORTANT RULES FOR GIVING TALKS

Scheduled time for talks at professional meetings generally varies from 10 to 30 minutes. Seminars and presentations at job interviews are usually longer—50 minutes (a class period) to 1 hour. Regardless of the time you have available, the general principles for giving talks are the same. And if you can master the 10-minute talk, you will have little trouble with longer talks, because the problem for most people is not finding enough to say but condensing what they have to say into the time allotted.

Two rules can help you prepare an effective oral presentation for any situation. First, *know the purpose of the talk*—why you are giving the talk and what you expect the audience to gain from it—*and communicate this purpose to the audience in your opening remarks*. The opening should answer the inevitable question in each listener's mind: "What's in it for me?" When a speech or seminar flops, the most common reason is that its purpose was not clear even to the speaker. Think about the message you want to get across, then carefully tailor your presentation of this message to the members of the audience—their education, age, experience, interests, and background in your subject area.

In most talks, the purpose is stated while attention is being drawn to the topic. In very informal settings or with a group very familiar with your topic, you can state the purpose at the outset. For example, in a departmental or graduate seminar you might simply say something like, "Today I'm going to tell you a little about the research I've been doing for the past 2 years in working toward my Ph.D. in biology." At the beginning of a meeting with your advisory committee, you might say, "To start our discussion, I'd like to summarize where I am in my work so far and what some of my main questions and problems are." Tell them what they are going to hear about and then follow through. If you want feedback—questions or discussion—from the audience throughout the talk or at the end, say so.

There is a formula you may have heard for giving a talk:

- First, tell them what you are going to tell them. (Give the purpose of your talk.)
- Then tell them. (Give the talk.)
- Then tell them what you told them. (Summarize main points.)

Many poor speakers start on methods, without stating the topic or explaining why the work was undertaken. An overemphasis on methods is one of the most common mistakes made in talks, especially by inexperienced researchers. Indeed, any talk that is not well thought out ahead of time usually emphasizes methods. (That's because everyone who does research knows what they did and how they did it, but not very many are as sure why they did it in the first place or what it all means in the end!)

To minimize this problem, devote only a relatively small portion of your allotted speaking time to the mechanics of the research. If, for example, you have 20 minutes total for your talk, spend the first 5 minutes introducing your topic, making sure your audience knows why you did the research. Spend the next 5 minutes explaining what you did (methods and results) and another 5 minutes summarizing your findings and their importance. This will leave 5 minutes for discussion, for questions and answers.

The second rule is, *keep the talk simple.* Just as your research objectives addressed only part of the larger problem area, your talk can only cover a part of your objectives. You cannot condense all your 2 to 4 years' work into 10 minutes, and it is both foolish and arrogant to try. Also, your listeners cannot go back over a difficult sentence or request that an inaudible one be repeated, and there are distractions in auditoriums that are usually not present when people read. So concentrate on concepts and eliminate confusing details. If members of the audience want to know the order in which you dissolved the various ingredients of your culture medium, they will ask you after the talk. Poor speakers nearly always present so much information that the listener becomes lost in a forest of details and cannot see the important points. The same criticism can hold for slides that obscure the point by including too much information.

An effective talk generally has only two to five main points, all of which relate to one main theme. All information presented should remind the hearer of the central theme. In a talk, the force of the impression upon the audience depends upon ruthless sacrifice of unnecessary detail.[3] Detail is acceptable only if it reinforces the main theme.

To test a talk you are listening to, ask yourself, "What is the point of the talk?" If you can figure out what the point is, and if the point seems of some relevance or importance, then it is a reasonably good talk. Bragg[3] said, "The success of the way in which the subject has been presented is measured by the extent to which the average member of the audience remembers it the next day." A really sucessful talk is thus one that you find yourself recounting or mentioning to others later on.

Most of this chapter concerns the sort of general research presentation you'd give in a departmental seminar or at a professional meeting. However, there are two types of oral presentation for which some additional information is needed. These are the final exam and the job seminar.

THE FINAL EXAMINATION, OR "THESIS DEFENSE"

As you finish writing your thesis, the time will approach for you to schedule your final oral examination. Schedule this exam only after all your committee members have had a chance to review your thesis, to discuss it with you individually, and to go over any substantial revisions you may have made to it. Don't schedule the exam if any member of the committee is obviously dissatisfied with the thesis. Once you have worked out any problems with your committee members and are close to having a final draft, you can feel relatively confident about a positive outcome from the final exam.

Although considerable preparation is necessary, this exam should not be regarded with undue anxiety or fear. All the work you have done on your thesis so far is preparation for this exam, as are the discussions you have had with your committee members about the thesis, and any prior talks you have given on your work at seminars or professional meetings. With the thesis almost complete, it may even be enjoyable to speak about what you have accomplished to a group of interested listeners.

Discuss the format of the exam with your advisor. Each advisor has his or her own preferred exam procedure, but you will probably be expected to start the session with a presentation on your project so that you can demonstrate your understanding of the research area and your ability to communicate what you have learned, as well as your ability to answer questions about it. A half hour is about average for this presentation.

Sometimes the exam is open to other faculty members and graduate students and sometimes it is "closed," or restricted only to you and your committee. Sometimes that atmosphere is formal and sometimes rather informal, but rarely is the student "grilled." The term "thesis defense" is misleading in this respect. It evokes images of you defending your thesis against attacks by outsiders. You do have to know what you are talking about, but after having worked on the project for many months, you ought to. The general tone of a final thesis exam, whether formal or informal, is usually rather cordial. If you have discussed criticisms of your thesis with each committee member and made a sincere effort to incorporate their suggested changes into your revision, it is unlikely that they will surprise you with new criticisms at the time of the exam. After the exam, recommended revisions of the thesis will probably range from correction of typographical errors to minor alterations of the text. Occasionally major revisions are required, but rarely, if ever, is the final exam failed outright.

Perhaps the best time to schedule the exam is 9 or 10 A.M. or 3 P.M. since this coincides with periods of minimum fatigue and hunger in adult human biorhythms (yours and your committee's). However, your foresight in providing coffee and perhaps donuts at one of these times would still be appreciated.

If the exam is open, your talk should include enough general elements to interest people who are not familiar with your project, but sufficient detail in appropriate areas to show the thoroughness of the work. Good visual aids and impeccable organization are essential. Your examiners will look for a certain polish and professionalism. Your job is to review the thesis in a way that invites questions and feedback from the group. Ideas generated at this exam can often be incorporated, if not into the thesis itself, into the publication that develops from it or into future research.

If the atmosphere is somewhat informal, people may interject questions during the talk, thus extending the time it will take you to cover your topic. In a more formal setting, questions may be asked only after you finish your presentation. As part of the questioning, each committee member may take up to 15 minutes to ask questions. In some exams, other graduate students may be asked to leave before formal questioning begins. This ritual tends to strike terror into the hearts of the graduate students who leave, giving them images of gruesome goings-on in the closed room behind them, but it *is* just a ritual and doesn't mean that things will happen that young people shouldn't see.

After about 2 hours even the most enthusiastic and well-prepared student will begin to fade, so rarely do oral examinations last longer than this. Some are shorter.

At the end of the exam, you will be asked to step outside the room while the committee discusses your performance. The length of their deliberations bears little relation to how well you did, though minutes may seem like hours as you stand outside and review all the things that you wish you'd said better or remembered when you were inside the exam room.

THE JOB INTERVIEW SEMINAR

When you become one of the top candidates for a job and are invited to be interviewed in person, you are usually expected—especially in academia—to give a seminar. The strategy for this is somewhat more complex than for a talk at a professional meeting. Consider who will come to hear your talk and why they are there. At a meeting, the topic is the center of attention. At a job seminar, you, not the topic, are the focus. You are being judged. In an academic setting, the audience will probably contain a number of faculty members, most of whom are from the department with the vacant position and are at least somewhat familiar with the general area of your research. A few will know a great deal about it. Also present will be graduate students and a few administrators, some of whom, like some of the attending faculty, will know very little about your research area.

During most of your allotted time in a job seminar, the same rules pertain as for other talks. You must present your subject in an understandable and interesting manner. You should avoid, as much as possible, arcane language and obscure details of methodology. You want your audience to like you, to see that you are enthusiastic about your work, and that you can communicate well. You will want to finish on schedule and allow time for discussion. If you are given an hour for the talk, speak for only 40 to 50 minutes.

In the job seminar, you will also want to demonstrate to the specialists in your area, and to the audience in general, that you are a really smart person who is extremely knowledgeable about the research area. The duration of the seminar—usually an hour—permits you to do this. At one or two points in your talk, take off. In an earnest and unpretentious manner go into some interesting details about some aspects of your research that will fascinate and impress a few of the people there but will lose the rest of your audience. But be sure to keep these phases of your talk relatively brief and keep coming back to a level for the general audience. Be sure to end with a clear and understandable summary. In the question-and-answer session, don't hesitate to give esoteric answers to esoteric questions, speaking directly, but briefly, to each questioner. But don't bluff when asked a question that is beyond your knowledge. Say that you do not know, but give an opinion if you can. Asking obscure or even unanswerable questions is one way employers sometimes test potential employees.

In a job interview, it is also very important to communicate your breadth of training and interests. This goal can be partly accomplished when you introduce your subject in the seminar. Show how your topic fits into a broad subject area. At the end of the talk, discuss the applications of your work, and stress the diversity of directions that it could take in the future.

PREPARATION

Controlling your very natural nervousness about speaking before a group, and projecting your knowledge and enthusiasm effectively, begin with being well prepared. Feeling confident about the organization and content of the talk, about appearance and arrangements, is the biggest step toward conquering stage fright. In preparing a talk, you must consider both *content* (the message you wish to convey), and *style* (how you will convey it). Most people spend more time on content than on style, but both are important, complementary aspects of any oral presentation.

The content of a research presentation can perhaps be best understood by reviewing the parts of the V outline described at the end of Chapter 3. In this chapter, emphasis is on style of presentation, and many suggestions are made on conveying your message effectively to an audience. I'm not sure that all these suggestions can be carried out in any single presentation, but an

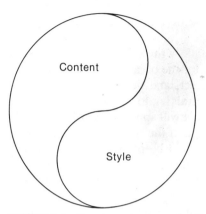

FIGURE 6-1   Complementary aspects of a talk.

attempt to follow most of them and, more important, to make each talk you give better than the one before, can help ensure that you deliver good talks.

There are four main ways in which a talk can be prepared and delivered. One is *memorization,* presenting the talk from memory with no notes. In general, this approach is not desirable. It's hard work and can sound stilted. Perhaps more important, memory may fail, especially when you are nervous, and without notes the temptation to talk to your slides is almost irresistible.

Some people *read* a talk from a prepared manuscript. This approach provides a great deal of security and helps some people talk without fumbling for words or saying "okay," "um," "uh," and "if you will" too often. But most people don't communicate well in this mode either. Because of the difference between the style needed for written versus spoken communication, a talk that is read aloud, word-for-word from a prepared text, can sound very boring and be hard to follow. It also prevents eye contact with the audience (like talking to your slides). The audience may feel disappointed in hearing you read a talk, thinking they should simply have obtained the manuscript and read it at home instead of wasting their time coming to the talk. Bragg[3] said that "to collect an audience and then read one's material is like inviting a friend to go for a walk and asking him not to mind if you go alongside him in your car."

If you want to read your talk, write it in the style of spoken words, in language appropriate for the occasion and the audience. The talk must be vigorous, direct, and personal. Write it from words said aloud as if you were talking to someone. Even if you are actually "reading" a paper that will appear in written form in a meeting proceedings, remember that the two modes of communication are very different and should be prepared and presented differently. For example, in most written accounts it is boring to be repetitious, while it is appropriate in a spoken account to put a key idea in several places to make sure the audience has grasped the point. And the written manuscript usually contains a great deal more detail than can be presented effectively at the actual talk. Simplify and clarify your material for oral presentation, saving details and lengthy explanations for the written report.

Most speakers give an *extemporaneous* talk. That is, notes or other memory aids are used, but ideas and information are not in their final words. The most common types of outline are the topic outline, the key-phrase outline, and the sentence outline, perhaps with key words highlighted or underlined. If you use notes, mark clearly where slides are to be changed. When you are concentrating on the talk, it is easy to forget to change slides, and this can be distracting for the audience. Carefully work out where to switch slides or to signal the projectionist. Sometimes it is effective to change slides right in the middle of a sentence so, as you say a key word or phrase, it is repeated and reemphasized by the slide. If a slide is shown more than once in your talk, have duplicates for that purpose rather than hope that you or the projectionist will be able to back up to an earlier slide.

I often outline a talk by thinking of the key slides that will tell the story. After the slides are thought out and slide copy has been prepared and sent off to be photographed, I work out the details to fill in around them. Preparing the slides first, as an outline, also helps scheduling, because you can have them made while you are working out the fine points of the talk.

An *impromptu* talk is one given completely off-the-cuff or ad-lib, without preparation. This is acceptable only if it is the only option, if no advance warning was received. Otherwise it is unforgivable. Even if you have only 5 minutes to prepare, you can jot down a couple of key points and extemporize from them. Most speakers outline an extemporaneous talk and then practice it aloud a few times, checking that it is within the allotted time limit. Then they use notes during the delivery.

SHORT-TERM PLANNING

Slides

As the time for giving a talk comes closer, attention shifts from content to style, and several items will require attention. For example, you should not assume that a projector will be provided. If you have to bring your own projector, make sure you bring extension cords and a spare projector lamp. If you have slides and a carousel projector will be used, bring the slides already placed into a carousel so that, regardless of whether a projectionist is present, the carousel can simply and quickly be put in place and you are assured that the slides are in the correct order and position. Purchase your own carousel ($5 to $9) if you can't borrow one easily.

Appearance

Consider what you are going to wear. Whether you like it or not, appearance counts heavily in preliminary judgments of you by professionals who do not know you. It affects how people listen to you, since it affects how serious you are perceived to be about your work. There is little sense in preparing a clear, effective talk with good visual aids, and then showing up in jeans and a cowboy shirt (or the local equivalent). Such behavior is considered an acceptable eccentricity, rather than an oversight, only in the brilliant and famous.

Staging

Other things to check the day of the talk include lighting and props. Never turn off all the lights to show slides. Even if subdued lighting detracts from your slides, insist that the room not be darkened entirely. You will need light to see your notes and to

CHECKLIST FOR A TALK

► 2 to 3 weeks ahead

- Outline talk
- List series of slides needed
- Sketch out wording and figures for slides
- Do (or have done) artwork

► 1 to 2 weeks ahead

- Make (or have made) slides
- Work out details of talk (especially opening and closing lines)
- Prepare notes to use during talk (mark slide changes, key words, pauses)
- Prepare introduction and give it to the moderator
- Find out if a projector will be provided

► 1 to 2 days ahead

- Practice talk aloud at least once and time it
- Practice opening and closing lines aloud
- Load carousel

► Day of talk

- Dress appropriately
- Practice opening and closing lines aloud
- Check out room, light switches, podium, podium light, projector, slide-change device, pointer, etc.

► Last minute

- Ask someone to switch lights off and on if needed
- Focus projector
- Put notes on podium
- Sit down and take several deep breaths

FIGURE 6-2

prevent your talk from coming from a disembodied voice in the dark.

Well-made slides can usually be seen in partial light. Negative slides with either a black or a dark-colored background can often be seen in a fairly well-lighted room. Although color slides of three-dimensional specimens or scenes are harder to see in the same light, you should minimize a distracting lights-off, lights-on approach. If your slides cannot be seen well with some lights on, make sure you have a strong podium light as well as, of course, a podium. You will need a podium to hold your notes in a readable but inconspicuous place. If possible, put your notes on the podium so you aren't carrying them when you walk up to give your talk. Check all other items you may need—a pointer and chalk, for example—and make sure they are in the room. Put the slide-change device, if there is one, in a convenient spot. Check the location and function of light switches.

A small, telescoping pocket pointer is handy to take to meetings, but try to develop a slide show in which you don't have to use a pointer in many slides. In a strange setting, using a pointer may be awkward and it makes you worry about one more thing when you are already nervous enough. In large meetings at conference centers, you may be provided with a flashlight pointer —one that projects an illuminated arrow wherever you point it. These are better in theory than in practice. Either the arrow is too dim to use effectively or, because of a magnification effect, your nervously shaking hand (unless it is well braced) produces an arrow that lurches maniacally across the screen. This is also true of overhead projectors; they magnify even normal hand tremors.

Don't expect to have a half hour to review your talk just before you give it. Despite the most careful planning, this opportunity rarely occurs. Before your session starts or during a previous lunch or coffee break, check out your slides to see that they are in focus and that they fill the screen without going over its edges. A focus slide (see page 134) can be used for this purpose. Finally, check out your podium light and turn it on. If necessary, find someone to turn the room lights off and on when you ask.

STARTING THE TALK

Introduction

The audience will need a brief background statement from you to understand who you are and why you are speaking to them. If someone is going to introduce you, prepare appropriate information, neatly typed, and give it to the introducer, preferably some time before the meeting. Offer to do this even if you haven't been asked. Not only is this a basic courtesy, since it saves the session moderator the trouble of extracting the information from you, but it assures that you will be introduced properly and with the sound of authority, not in a way that starts your talk on the wrong foot. If your name or any other words in the introduction are hard to pronounce, write them phonetically so the introducer will not trip over them. You may include any pertinent information that you feel fits the occasion. If the moderator or introducer wants to change it, he or she can, but usually few changes are made. If no one is going to introduce you, introduce yourself. Don't just start giving the talk.

Opening Lines

It is very important to appear confident in the opening moments of your talk. Spend time thinking about how to introduce your subject effectively and the exact words you will use. Practice your opening lines. If necessary, memorize them for authority. This will help get you through any initial nervousness, as it is easier to extemporize well from notes once you have warmed up.

Never begin your talk without first establishing audience contact. Before you say a word, pause and look directly at several friendly people. Smile. If possible, say at least one or two opening lines before lights are dimmed for slides. Opening directly with a statement of purpose is appropriate in the rare case when your audience has a genuine interest or a thorough knowledge of your topic (such as in a committee meeting or in a classroom lecture). In most other situations, you must first attract and focus attention on the topic. The benefit or relationship of the topic to the audience must be communicated. This link may be critical in getting your topic across. Research has shown that the most effective teachers and speakers are the ones who start by saying something to bring the audience into their subject in a personal way. For example, "I realize that there aren't many crocodiles in Idaho, but. . . ." Another strategy is to start by presenting some of the questions that people commonly ask you about your work. A striking slide and a question ("Have you ever seen . . . and wondered what causes it?") are often effective.

Attention can also be obtained in other ways. Speech books suggest a quote, a rhetorical question, or a startling statement. Use one of these techniques if you feel comfortable doing so, but avoid jokes. Very, very few people can start a talk effectively with a joke. Even if the joke is funny, it rarely relates to the topic in a useful way. And for some reason, the joke that convulses friends over a beer tends to suffer as it emerges through an amplifying system. (More subtle humor throughout a talk can, however, be appropriate and effective.)

Apologies

No apologies are allowed when giving talks, except under the direst circumstances. Don't say that you didn't prepare adequately. Your apology may make you feel better but you will lose the sympathy of your audience. They don't want their time wasted by a poorly prepared speaker. Apologizing for being unprepared says, to your audience, that either you are very unprofessional or that you think that they are pretty small potatoes and are not worth much effort. That is probably not the message that you want to convey. Even if your listeners think your talk was poor, they should think you did the best you could for them. Incompleteness of data and/or inconclusiveness of results are not fatal flaws if presented in a positive, undogmatic manner.

Don't apologize for poor slides or speaking with an accent either. Instead of an apology, a slide with extraneous material on it necessitates a lunge at the screen, by you, with a pointer. This display of energy can save the day as you briskly point to what you want the audience to see and lead them through the material as clearly as you can. If you speak with an accent, use visual aids with words to repeat key words and ideas. Word slides are particularly important at international meetings. They ensure that what you say is heard correctly.

Keep a bold front at all times. Don't magnify your mistakes. If they are small, don't point them out. You would be amazed at what people *don't* see if it is not pointed out to them. The flaws that you perceive in your presentation, if you have some know-how and fairly high standards, will probably not be noticed by 99 percent of your audience. If a major problem occurs, such as a coughing fit or a problem with the projector, correct the situation as best you can in a quiet, professional manner, and then go back to your presentation.

DURING THE TALK

Speak slowly and clearly and avoid the temptation to add detail. Show enthusiasm about your topic, and talk to the audience, not to your slides or to your notes. If slide-changing is as carefully thought out as it should be, there will be no need for you to look at your own slides, except to check occasionally and quickly that you are projecting the right one or to point out something important. Don't use your slides for notes. Our culture expects honest people to have eye contact with the people to whom they are talking. Eye contact also helps you hold the listeners' attention.[22] You can note their reactions and adapt. When you sense confusion, you can amplify a point. When you sense boredom, you can move along more quickly.

In your first experiences in talking before a group—when you are nervous and worried about your slides, words, and just getting through it alive—establishing eye contact may be difficult. Nevertheless, because it is important, you should start trying to incorporate it into your talks. While speaking, slowly look around the room, completing each thought while looking at a different person. Avoid scanning without really seeing the audience. Pause slightly between paragraphs or ideas. (A series of dots in your notes can remind you to do this.)

If you use a pointer during your talk, be precise in your movements. Don't gesture vaguely at the screen. Clearly indicate the word, number, line, or other item that you want the audience to pay attention to, then *put the pointer down.*

In a research talk, you should integrate discussion and results. Never present these two items separately as you would in a written report. Emphasize applications and generalizations that can be drawn from your work.

ENDING THE TALK

Keep track of time. Put your watch or a small clock on the podium right next to your notes. If there is a session moderator, you might ask him or her to tell you when you have, for example, 5 minutes left. If you wish, mark sections toward the end of your notes that can be dropped if time runs short, but don't drop your closing lines.

A well-thought-out ending is as important as a strong beginning. The final minute of the talk will strongly affect how people will remember you. Present conclusions in a way that invites comments and discussion, then end the talk decisively. Don't soften your voice or speed up on the last point you make. Don't fade out as you finish. After you say your last sentence, switch to a blank slide (see page 134) and say "Thank you." (Put THANK YOU in block letters at the end of your notes.) This tells the audience that you have finished the talk. Pause slightly (the audience may clap) then turn toward the moderator. The moderator is generally the one who asks for questions. If the moderator makes no move to do this, or if there is no moderator, ask for questions yourself.

The question period is a big worry for most inexperienced speakers. You imagine that all questions will be directed, with malice, at the very areas that you are unsure of. The probability that this will happen is very small. In fact, after worrying themselves to a frazzle about this, most graduate students are disappointed that the questions are so elementary and give them so little chance to show what they know. If your worst fears come true in a public presentation, it is sometimes helpful to realize that the person who seems to be picking on you—pointing out an obvious oversight, or suggesting that the work might better have been done another way—is usually not trying to make you look dumb, but to make himself or herself look smart. Defensiveness is both inappropriate and unnecessary. Bluffing rarely succeeds, but abject confessions of ignorance are not required either. If a courteous and informative answer is not possible, you need simply say "That's a good point," or "I hadn't thought about that." If someone persists in a difficult line of questioning, express an interest in continuing discussion of the subject *after* your talk.

More disheartening, perhaps, is being faced with total silence in response to your—or the moderator's—request for questions. One question is usually all it takes to get an audience started in discussion. You might consider furnishing a friend with a question that you would like to be asked if questioning starts slowly.

An audience becomes hostile when a speaker goes overtime, even if the talk or follow-up discussion is very good. They feel trapped. (If there is a following speaker, going overtime is an inexcusable discourtesy.) Conversely, audiences and session moderators love a speaker who finishes slightly under time. A good speaker normally presents no more than the equivalent of one double-spaced typed page in 2 to 3 minutes. Thus, a 10-minute talk, if completely written out, would be only four pages long. Don't be fooled as you rehearse. It takes considerably longer to deliver a talk effectively in front of a group than to simply read it aloud.

Your time may run out when questions and discussion are still lively. If there is pressure of a following speaker or a need to vacate the room, simply say, "I see that my time is up. Thank you again." If you can stay, invite people with other commitments to leave. This strategy leaves you with the smaller group that is most interested in your topic. In any case, be prepared to stay for a while, inside or outside the room, to talk to those most interested in your work.

REPEATING A TALK

If you wish to repeat a talk that you've given before, go over your notes and slides carefully, reworking them for freshness and greater clarity. Even if only a few days or weeks have elapsed since you last gave the talk, don't simply dust off your notes, put the carousel into the projector and repeat the same talk verbatim. No matter how much preparation you put into the talk the first time, it will come across as stale and unenthusiastic if the work is not very clear and fresh in your mind. You can always improve a talk, and if you don't make the effort, it will be worse than the first time you gave it.

Visual Aids

An effective talk should be simple and interesting, with a purpose and main points that are clear to the audience. Visual aids of various kinds can help you achieve this goal. Visual aids most commonly used are:

1 *Slide transparencies* (or slides): These may be positive—looking like the original material (black-and-white or colored, showing lettering, drawings, or photographs of three-dimensional specimens, equipment, or scenes), negative (either black or dark-colored background with white detail), or color-augmented negative (white detail hand-colored in different ways for emphasis).

2 *Overhead transparencies* (viewgraphs or overheads): These are either handwritten or photocopied onto acetate sheets. Some computer-linked graphics systems can be used to plot graphs directly onto transparencies.

3 *Handouts*: You might distribute photocopies, mimeos, dittos, and so on.

4 *Blackboard* or *flip-chart*.

Slides are usually the best choice for professional meetings or any presentation you consider particularly important. Negative slides (especially those with a blue background) are often considered superior to positive slides because they can be seen in a half-lighted room, and the figure itself, not the background, dominates the viewer's vision. Overheads, blackboards, and flip-charts are usually more suitable for small informal groups than for large audiences or important talks. The main disadvantage of overheads is that handling them is often awkward and the projector, being in the front of the room, interferes with the audience's view of both the speaker and the screen. Using both slides and transparencies in a single presentation can be distracting. Unless separate screens are used and use of each is well-rehearsed, the speaker will appear (and usually is) ill-prepared.

To effectively keep the interest of your audience, most material presented on a blackboard or flip-chart should be drawn up ahead of time. If you do write during the presentation, stop talking when you turn away from the audience. Handouts are generally provided when the speaker wishes the audience to take home some specific information, such as details of methodology or a reference list. Using handouts to outline your talk is not particularly desirable since they compete for audience attention.

PURPOSES OF VISUAL AIDS

Visual aids can reinforce important points by repetition. Visual aids should repeat visually, in pictures and words, the important points of your talk. At times, slides with single key words can be particularly effective. If you have four main points, you need at least four slides, one for each point, plus a topic or title slide and a summary slide for the end. If you are giving a standard research presentation, a minimum set of slides might be:

Topic
Main questions or problem statement
Objectives
Approach used (simple outline or flow chart)
Results (a graph or figure is better than a table)
Conclusions

Avoid the common error of omitting the closing slide. Depending upon your audience and your purpose, this slide may summarize main points, make recommendations, stress benefits, or call for action.

Sensory repetition of your main points is an important consideration. When you use visual aids, the audience both hears and sees your main points. But there are three other senses as well—touch, smell, and taste—and you can introduce any or all of these to get your main points across. Sometimes it is appropriate, in a smaller group, to pass something around (adding touch). Sometimes an item with a characteristic smell can be passed around. Even referring to impressions of touch, taste, or smell can effectively stimulate the audience's imagination and interest.

Visual aids can be used to simplify and clarify an idea. Some ideas or activities are very difficult to explain without losing the audience's interest. In such cases, a picture is indeed worth a thousand words. However, visual aids can simplify or clarify only if they themselves are simple and clear. *A primary rule for slides is that each should present only one central idea.* The most common error in using slides is having too much information on single slides. The error is compounded if printing is small and faint. This makes it diffiuclt for the audience to quickly understand the point being made, and the audience loses interest. Use several simple slides rather than one complicated one, especially if you plan to discuss something at length. If you must show a complex slide—for example, a diagram or a flow chart—show it first to provide a general perspective, then show one or more additional slides to amplify details shown in the first slide (Figure 6-3).

If you wish to show a map of a local area, first show a map of a larger area (such as the entire United States) with a dot or square and a big arrow pointing out the site of interest. Subsequent slides could focus upon the site itself (Figure 6-4).

Because of the greater inconvenience and time involved in changing overheads, and because overheads are generally used in a smaller room with the audience closer to the screen, more information can be included in these. But efforts must be made to keep the relationships between your spoken words and the overhead clear. To do this, you may wish to circle or draw arrows to portions of the projected material as you speak, or to cover the overhead with an opaque piece of paper and progressively disclose information as you move through you presentation. This same technique of progressive disclosure can be used effectively with slides (Figure 6-5).

Visual aids can be used to add interest. Sensory repetition is important here. The key, of course, is getting the audience involved in your topic in as many ways as possible. Our ability to

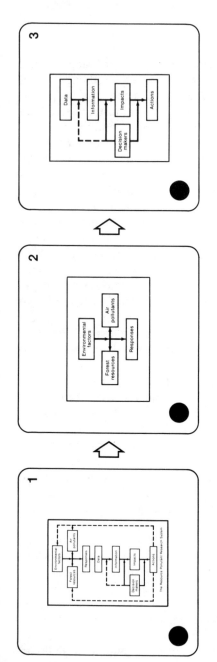

FIGURE 6-3 Sequential focus on parts of a complex slide.

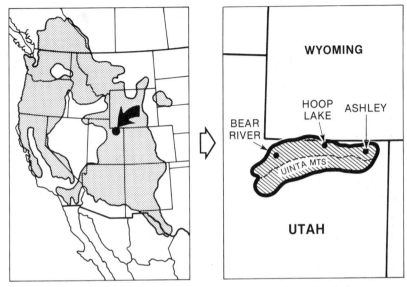

FIGURE 6-4   Progressive detail in a series of slides to show a local site.

filter out sounds (stereo music, voices, and so on) and to relegate
them to background noise so that we can think about other things
is very well developed and often difficult to control or override.
The more senses your listeners use during the course of your talk,
the less likely they are to lose interest.

The audience's interest in a slide lasts only a few seconds. A
simple slide reinforcing a single idea, word, or point might be
projected for only 2 to 3 seconds. If you want your audience to stay
interested in a single slide for more than a few seconds, you either
have to point things out on it or break it up into several slides, each
focusing upon a single aspect of the material (Figure 6-6). Some
slides may be left on longer, but there is rarely an excuse for
projecting a slide for more than a minute. (If a single slide contains
so much information that it must remain on the screen for longer
than that, it is probably a poor slide.) One slide per minute of your
talk (not counting the discussion period) would be a minimum.
Experienced speakers may show 50 or more slides in a half-hour

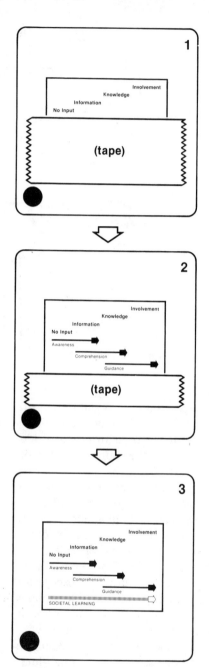

FIGURE 6-5 Progressive disclosure of information on consecutive replicate slides.

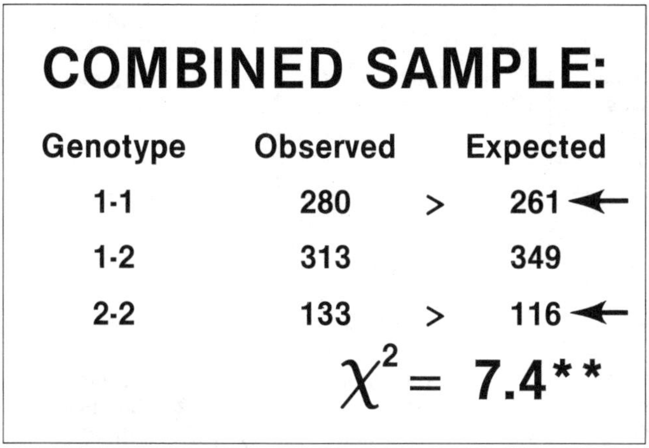

COMBINED SAMPLE:

Genotype	Observed		Expected
1-1	280	>	261 ←
1-2	313		349
2-2	133	>	116 ←

$$\chi^2 = 7.4**$$

FIGURE 6-6   Use arrows or circles to highlight important points.

talk. A transparency generally has more information on it than a slide and can therefore be left on the screen longer.

Visual aids can help the audience follow an organized plan of presentation. The organization of your talk should be obvious to the audience. A simple outline, developing progressively as you talk, helps your listeners keep track of where you are. Sometimes it is effective to show the whole list first, when you tell the audience what you are going to talk about. Then progressively build the list, starting with the first item as you go into the talk itself (Figure 6-7).

PREPARING ILLUSTRATIONS

The simplest and best way to prepare illustrations for a thesis, publication, or talk is to discuss your ideas with a graphic artist and have the illustrations made professionally. This approach is strongly recommended for a talk at a professional meeting or at a job interview. However, if you are new at the game, as well as impoverished or in a hurry, this option may not be available. Fortunately, there are a great many publications and experienced people available to help you prepare your own illustrations, and there are many shortcuts that can save you time and money

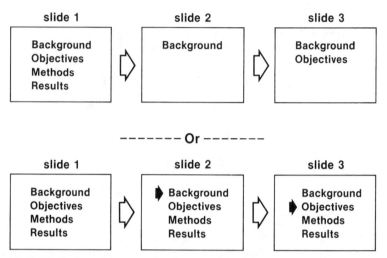

FIGURE 6-7   Use slides to outline the organization of the talk for the audience.

without significantly reducing the quality of the final product. You know by now what visual aids are supposed to do. While technical perfection is wonderful, visual aids can be technically spectacular but still not communicate your point effectively. Know what message you want your visual aids to convey. If they do that, technical perfection is not essential. The important thing is that they communicate your message and that their appearance is professional—clear and neat—and doesn't distract the audience from understanding the message.

The following discussion focuses on preparation of slides from line drawings, tables, or text, but most of the techniques and principles can be applied to other types of illustrations, including thesis figures. There are three stages to making slides. First is deciding what you want them to show (discussed earlier in this chapter). Next is doing the artwork (or making slide "copy"). Last is making the slides themselves from the original artwork. This whole process takes at least 2 to 3 weeks unless you do all of it yourself. Procrastination can get you into real trouble.

Simplify   Simplification is the key to success, especially with slides. An entire typewritten page or published table will not make an effective slide. Simplify the material or break it down into several slides. Better yet, avoid tables entirely. Present your data as bar charts, pie diagrams, histograms, or graphs, and keep them simple (Figure 6-8).

You should be able to read your finished slides without a magnifier. Wording or numbers must not be crowded. The maximum size of typed material is about the size of a 3 x 5 inch file card, centered on an 8½ x 11 inch sheet of paper (Figure 6-9).

If you take a diagram from a book or article, first photocopy it, then simplify it to suit your purposes by whiting out portions of

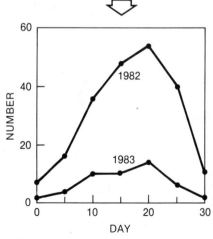

Number of adult moths collected in 10 sweeps

Day	1982	1983
0	8	2
5	16	4
10	36	10
15	48	10
20	54	14
25	40	6
30	10	2

FIGURE 6-8 Graphs are more effective than tables.

M A X I M U M   S I Z E   of typed area for a slide

is about the size of a 3 x 5 inch file card.

● Any more typing than this on a slide will be
   too small to be seen at the back of the room.

● Use a good electric typewriter with carbon
   ribbon.

● Keep the text as simple as possible.

● Use UPPER CASE, S P A C I N G, and <u>underlining</u>
   to add emphasis to important points.
   Rub-on arrows, dots, etc., also look good.

FIGURE 6-9

it (legends, footnotes, fine lines and excessive detail), darkening some lines, and adding enlarged words or arrows for emphasis (Figure 6-10). It is almost never appropriate to include the published figure or table legend in a slide. The words "Figure 4" must be taken out and the legend simplified and enlarged. Even if it *is* the fourth figure you've shown, this information is irrelevant to your audience. (Worse yet is a slide in which a page number appears!) Five or fewer words are usually best for a slide heading or legend. A one-word heading is ideal if it communicates the message.

Trace   Another technique to help you simplify and strengthen published illustrations and maps, especially for slides, is tracing. With drafting tape (like masking tape), attach a copy of the picture to a table and tape a piece of good-quality tracing

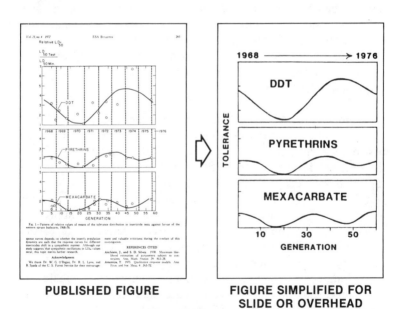

PUBLISHED FIGURE   **FIGURE SIMPLIFIED FOR SLIDE OR OVERHEAD**

FIGURE 6-10   Simplify published material to make a slide. (*Source: Savin, N. E., J. L. Robertson, and R. M. Russell, A Critical Evaluation of Bioassay in Insecticide Research: Likelihood Ratio Tests of Dose-mortality Regression, Bull. Entomol. Soc. Am., 23(4):257–266, 1977.*)

paper over it. Then go at the picture with a ruler and a set of new black felt-tip pens of different widths. White correcting fluid can be used to fix your mistakes. Relative darkness of lines highlights important features of the picture. Leave out extraneous lines and make important lines much darker than on the original. In any figure, be sure that the boldest (darkest and widest) line is the line you want the audience to notice first. In a graph, the boldest line should be the curve, not the x and y axes. In a map, a state or county boundary, a distributional area for a species, or a single site might be emphasized.

Enlarge   Don't make any picture the size it must appear when finished, even in your thesis. Enlarge the picture you want to trace via a photocopy or a photographic process. Alternatively, project the picture, with an opaque projector or a "map-o-graph," onto a clean piece of paper and draw on the projected image only what you want in the slide. The bigger and bolder you make your tracing, the better it will look reduced as a figure in your thesis or as a slide or overhead. Imperfections in the larger drawing will disappear in reduction, giving the picture a cleaner and more professional look.

Label   Finally, label your figure or graph boldly. Minimum letter height is one-twenty-fifth the illustration height. Unless you first reduce the unlabeled figure to about 3 x 5 inches, typing on the figure will be too small for the audience to read. Instead, use a tape letterer (such as Kroy), an ink-lettering set (such as a Leroy set, though using this takes practice), or press-on lettering (readily available in most university bookstores but difficult to apply in a straight line). If you do use Kroy or press-on lettering, tape your figure over a sheet of graph paper and use the lines to help you apply the lettering straight. Alternatively, if you will use black and white film, draw guidelines on the figure itself with a T square and nonreproducing blue pencil, or prepare the entire figure on graph paper with light, nonreproducing blue guidelines.

Add Emphasis and Shading   When photographing three-dimensional objects, show relative size with, for example, a pointing finger, a ruler, or some other familiar object. You can also use cutout paper arrows to indicate parts of interest within the photo. There are even techniques for applying arrows and simple captions or labels to finished slides. For line drawings, press-on arrows and shading film (parallel lines or dots) are extremely handy and effective. Gray areas do not reproduce well in photocopies or with high-contrast film (the kind of film you will want to use for crisp graphs and figures). For publication, solid grays necessitate a half-tone printing process that is considerably more costly than black-and-white only. Use the boldest dots or parallel lines that still produce the appropriate effect. Don't choose excessively fine shading film or, if you are shading by hand, don't stipple or cross-hatch with too delicate a touch.

Reduce and Copy   For a thesis illustration, reduce the finished figure or graph with a reducing photocopy machine or a photographic process. Unless they are very large, drawings for slides do not have to be reduced before they are photographed. Any artwork that is shiny or has edges or texture that might produce undesirable shadows (such as Kroy lettering tape), should be photocopied and the photocopy used to make the slide or overhead.

Word Slides

Word or data slides must be simple—15 to 20 words per slide is recommended. Have no more than 10 to 15 numbers on a data slide. In general, include no more data than you are going to discuss. If you do, use arrows, circles, or other highlighting to indicate the numbers you will discuss (Figure 6-6).

Because it is convenient and fast, typing is often used instead of commercial lettering. To make typed slides, use an electric typewriter with a carbon ribbon and white bond paper. Typed slides prepared this way are perfectly acceptable, as long as the typed area is small enough, the lettering dark enough, and the photograph taken so that the writing nearly fills the image area of the finished slide.

Lettering bolder than typing, however, looks better in slides and is more clearly visible to the audience. It looks professional and "crisp." Unless typing is very dark and photographed just right, it tends to look off-white in negative slides. Word slides can be typeset from many word processors or with facilities found at any newspaper office and many copy-machine businesses. However, if you don't do your own photography of the typeset material, slides can cost up to $2 each. If the talk you are going to give is important to you—a job seminar or an important professional meeting, for example—$2 per slide may not be too high. If such technical perfection is not necessary, you can make slides nearly as attractive and effective with Kroy lettering or a Leroy lettering set. Unless you have a supply on hand, press-on lettering is *not* recommended for word slides because it is difficult to apply straight and is relatively expensive.

Similar procedures can be used for overheads, but because overheads are used for smaller and more informal groups, they can also be lettered neatly by hand. If the room is small and everyone is going to be close to the screen, large typing (as with IBM Orator) is acceptable. If you use Orator, be sure to use 10 rather than 12 characters per inch (Figure 6-11).

Photographing Your Artwork

Slides made from your own artwork cost from about 50 cents to $1 each, regardless of whether you photograph them yourself. Most universities have a facility on campus to produce slides from original artwork, and your research budget can be used to cover the cost. It is not particularly difficult, however, to photograph your own artwork for slides, although by the time you take enough pictures to work out the correct exposure, this approach may be more expensive in the long run.

Ideally, all text, figure, or data slides in one talk should be of the same type. It can be distracting to your audience if you mix, for example, positive and negative slides or blue and black background slides. Mixing slides of text, drawings, and actual specimens or scenes, however, is desirable.

IBM ORATOR TYPED 12 LETTERS PER INCH IS TOO CROWDED.

ORATOR TYPED 10 LETTERS PER INCH LOOKS BETTER.

FIGURE 6-11

Use a 35-mm single-lens reflex camera with a lens that focuses as close as 10 to 12 inches. Macro lenses, macro-zoom lenses, close-up filters, and extension tubes will all allow close focusing. However, if you make very big artwork (larger than 12 x 18 inches or so), you can take pictures without special lenses. Simply lay your picture down under adequate lighting, mount your camera on a tripod, and go to it. Cameras and appropriate lenses can usually be borrowed from your advisor or another person in your department or university. Similarly, most departments have available a copy stand for taking pictures. A copy stand provides the needed evenness of light over the entire copy area. An alternative is to photograph outdoors in diffused light (such as in even shade or on an overcast day). Film type should match the lighting—tungsten film for tungsten lights on a copy stand, daylight film for natural light.

To make black-and-white slides from line drawings, use a high-contrast negative film—one that makes darks white and whites dark—such as Kodak's Kodalith. With such film, tape, erasures, and other corrections won't show up in the slide. The negative itself can be used as a slide with a black background. If you cannot find a good high-contrast negative film, be sure that the artwork you copy is very clean—free from anything that will show up as gray and look messy in the finished slide.

Continuous-tone black-and-white film (such as Kodak's Panatomic-X) or color film (such as Ektachrome) is more readily available than high-contrast film and is appropriate for photographing very clean line drawings or three-dimensional specimens or artwork where shades of gray are acceptable or must be seen. If you are in a big hurry, use a Polaroid system (with either high-contrast or continuous-tone film) to make your slides.

Negative slides with colored backgrounds are attractive and effective. Many speakers prefer a dark blue background. To make such slides, there are now several convenient and inexpensive alternatives to the old diazo process. Photographing black-and-white drawings with Kodak Ektachrome 64 with a yellow filter gives white detail on a blue field when it is commercially processed by what is called C-41 processing. This type of processing is readily available and can often be done within a single day.

MAKING BLUE-BACKGROUND SLIDES WITH WHITE LETTERS

Materials

35-mm camera with light meter

Ektachrome 64 slide film (daylight professional)

K2 or #8 yellow filter (screw-on or gelatin)

Photo stand (copy stand) with daylight blue bulbs. (Note: Ektachrome 64 slide film (Tungsten, 3200K) with tungsten bulbs will give the same results.) If you don't have a copy stand, outdoor light and a steady hand will work almost as well.

Method

Set camera ASA setting to 80.

Expose as the meter reads. (Note: Film is cheap, time is not.) "Bracket" each shot. That is, overexpose each subject one f-stop and underexpose one f-stop. This gives you a range of exposures to choose from if your camera's light meter is inaccurate, or if f-stops and/or shutter speeds are not exact, or if you have different preferences for shading.

Take film to a local photo shop for developing. Specifically request that the film be processed by the C-41 print process, and that the results be mounted as slides. (Note: 24-hour turnaround is usually available, but don't count on it.)

Variations

If you prefer different colors, use a different filter or combination of filters. The background will come out the complementary color and brightness of the filter used. For example, a light blue filter will produce a deep red background; light green produces magenta.

FIGURE 6-12

Framing

Whatever film you use, be sure to frame the picture closely. The best-prepared material is ruined if it is photographed too far away, with a margin too big and letters too small. Because the camera usually sees about 5 percent more than you see through the viewfinder, shoot close to the borders of your artwork so that unwanted background does not end up around the edges of your finished slide (Figure 6-13).

You can mount slides yourself by any of a number of techniques. There are several types of quick cardboard mounts that simply require you to cut out your film, position it in the mount, and then heat-seal the edges with an iron. These cardboard mounts are satisfactory for most purposes, since most of your

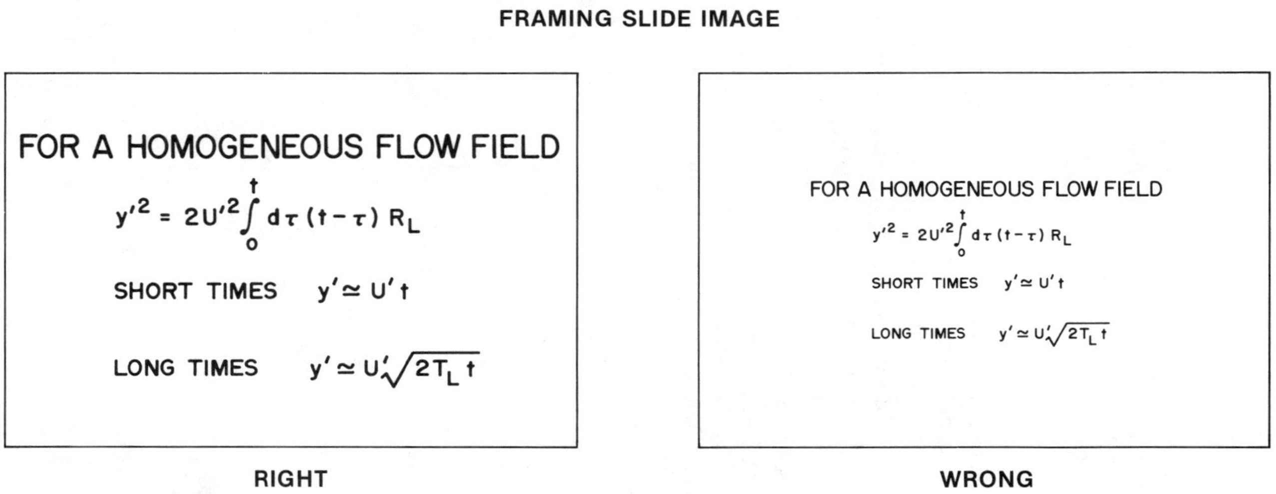

FRAMING SLIDE IMAGE

FOR A HOMOGENEOUS FLOW FIELD

$$y'^2 = 2U'^2 \int_0^t d\tau (t-\tau) R_L$$

SHORT TIMES $y' \simeq U't$

LONG TIMES $y' \simeq U' \sqrt{2T_L t}$

RIGHT

FOR A HOMOGENEOUS FLOW FIELD

$$y'^2 = 2U'^2 \int_0^t d\tau (t-\tau) R_L$$

SHORT TIMES $y' \simeq U't$

LONG TIMES $y' \simeq U' \sqrt{2T_L t}$

WRONG

FIGURE 6-13   Photograph image close up to eliminate extraneous margins.

slides will be used only a few times. For slides that will be reused extensively, plastic snap-together or metal rims can be used. Some of the fancier mounting systems include a thin glass plate on either side of the film, but such glass mounts distort focus unless special flat-field projection lenses are used.

Handling

As you make each slide, draw a conspicuous round dot—a "thumbprint"—in the lower left-hand corner of the mount (Figure 6-14). This dot will make it much easier and quicker to put your slides in the carousel properly. Number the slides in order if you wish, but use pencil so you can neatly change the order in subsequent presentations.

Carry your slides with you on your trip. Don't trust them to baggage if you check it through. You could give your talk in your travelling clothes, but without the slides you would be in big trouble. The carousel itself might go with the suitcase, but keep

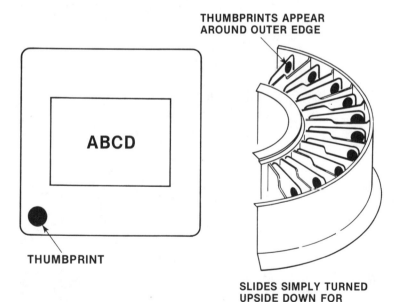

FIGURE 6-14 Orienting slides for placement in carousel.

the slides in your pocket or briefcase. (In some situations, it is not excessively cautious to bring two sets of slides—one in your briefcase, for example, and the other in your pocket.) Using clear plastic slide files permits you to easily review the slides as you go over the talk one last time and put the slides in the carousel (Figure 6-15).

Mark your carousel—not just the box it goes in—clearly with your name, address, talk number, and title on masking tape. This will help the projectionist show the right set of slides at the right time. Also, in the discussion following a talk, speakers often leave without their slides. Having the carousel labeled will help ensure that you get the slides back eventually.

No matter how well prepared you are, there will still be times when you have no slide to illustrate what you are talking about. In such cases, it is important that the audience is not left looking at a projected slide that is not related to what you are saying. You could leave an empty space in the carousel. However, if your listeners have been looking at slides with dark backgrounds, they will suddenly be bathed in bright light from the screen. This could serve the useful purpose of waking up some people, but it isn't

FIGURE 6-15 Plastic slide files are handy for carrying, viewing, and storing slides.

optimal staging. An alternative is to use an opaque or "blank" slide at crucial points. Some of the newer projectors have a built-in blank slide. Wherever there is no slide in a slot in the carousel, an opaque flap prevents light from projecting onto the screen. If you are not using such a projector, you could simply insert 2 x 2 inch squares of stiff tagboard or construction paper in appropriate slots in the carousel. Alternatively, you can cut the paper smaller and mount it just like your other slides. A blank slide should be inserted after the last slide in your talk.

To make a focus slide to check the projection system before your talk, simply poke a tiny pinhole in the opaque paper in each corner of the picture area of a blank slide. With this slide, you can unobstrusively check your focus and see that the image area fills the screen without slopping over. If some of your slides have the long dimension positioned vertically, use two focus slides, one rotated 90 degrees, to assure proper positioning of the pictures on the screen.

To facilitate handling of overheads, each transparent sheet can be taped to a lightweight cardboard frame (available for about 30¢ each). These frames prevent the annoying problem of overheads sticking together. Also, you can write on them, so you can clearly label each one.

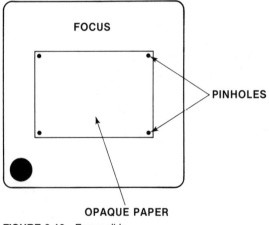

FIGURE 6-16 Focus slide.

Chapter 7

Writing about Research

In doing your research, you will progressively narrow your work from a general topic to a specific problem to a final thesis. In formal terms, a thesis is a belief about a topic that you will support or refute with evidence in your report (which is then called a thesis). In essence, your written thesis is the final version of your hypothesis, with all the trappings of the rational model of research attached.

When you set about writing your thesis in earnest, you take your findings, assess their implications, then reconstruct the whole process whereby you arrived at them, and begin writing. For obvious reasons, this reconstruction is necessary for communicating the essentials of your work as concisely and clearly as possible, but it should be equally obvious that the written account of the completed research will be quite different from the way the research was actually done. Writing a thesis is an exercise in organization or, more precisely, reorganization. Your aim is to demonstrate that you have learned how to do original research and that you know how to communicate your discoveries to others.

The thesis, like a journal article, contains an introduction, methods, results, and discussion. These standardized headings ensure that the contents can be understood quickly and easily by the reader:

> What was the problem? (Introduction)
> How did you study the problem? (Methods)
> What did you find? (Results)
> What do these findings mean? (Discussion)

Unlike a journal article, however, the thesis may describe more than one topic and may present more than one approach to some topics. The thesis may also include an account of some of the imaginative processes that the student went through in arriving at his or her discoveries. The introduction often includes a statement of hypotheses as well as a series of objectives, and may contain an extensive and detailed literature review, something rarely found in a journal article. Methods and results sections are sometimes extremely detailed. The thesis often tells what *didn't* work as well as what did, and gives sufficient detail so that successful approaches can be replicated by someone else. The thesis may present all or most of the data obtained in the thesis research. Therefore, the thesis is often longer and more involved than a scientific paper. Perhaps the greatest similarity between a thesis and a journal article is in the discussion, where the significance of the findings is presented and generalizations are made.

Graduate schools vary as to whether a research paper (submitted for publication or actually published) can be substituted for a thesis. On one hand, the writing of a thesis can be viewed as an academic exercise aimed at helping the student carefully think through and unravel his or her first research project. The writing of a lengthy report may aid the advisor and committee in evaluating the quality of the work the student did, regardless of the broad significance of the discoveries he or she made. On the other hand, it is often argued that students who learn how to write a thesis don't necessarily get any training in the actual publication process. Since research has little value unless it is communicated, and because a journal article will reach a much larger audience than a thesis will, a publication in a refereed journal is a superior demonstration of a student's ability to both do and communicate research than is a thesis. However, because there is a lag of up to a year or more between submission of a manuscript and its acceptance by a journal, some institutions compromise and simply require that the manuscript be prepared as ready to submit to a particular journal.

WRITING STYLE

A research report should communicate information as accurately and concisely as possible. The less energy your readers waste on decoding your language, the more they'll have left for your brilliant ideas.[10] Remember that your prime purpose is to explain something, not to prove you are smarter than your readers. Your aim is to be read, understood, and remembered. Good writing is characterized by correct and simple sentence structure, effective and lucid word choices, use of topic sentences, avoidance of jargon, and elegant simplicity of expression.[25] Nevertheless, many articles in technical journals—even journals with the highest standards for quality of research presented—are poorly written. Woodford[30] said:

> Some of the worst are produced by the kind of author who consciously pretends to a "scientific scholarly" style. He takes what should be lively, inspiring, and beautiful and, in an attempt to make it seem dignified, chokes it to death with stately abstract nouns; next, in the name of scientific impartiality, he fits it with a complete set of passive constructions to drain away any remaining life's blood or excitement; then he embalms the remains in molasses of polysyllable, wraps the corpse in an impenetrable veil of vogue words, and buries the stiff old mummy with much pomp and circumstance in the most distinguished journal that will take it. Considered either as a piece of scholarly work or as a vehicle of communication, the product is appalling.

To write clearly, you must *want* to write clearly. You must also be willing to work hard—to revise and revise and revise. And you must follow some basic guidelines. Helpful suggestions for the appropriate writing style for a thesis or a scientific journal article are provided in numerous references. Particularly useful are Strunk and White's classic, *The Elements of Style*,[28] and Robert Day's *How to Write and Publish a Scientific Paper*;[8] Richard Davis's *Thesis Projects in Science and Engineering*[7] provides details for writing engineering reports.

Here are some particularly important bits of advice for writing a thesis:

Use precise words and expressions Avoid ambiguity and vagueness:

> Depth contours will be plotted with a sounding device. (Why not a pen or pencil?)
> Manageable (In what respect?)
> Affect (Reduce? Increase?)
> Large (How large?)
> Severe (How severe? Severe in what way?)

E. B. White warned, "When you say something, make sure you have said it. The chances of your having said it are only fair." If you use an abstract term (like "large"), follow it with concrete examples or terms (such as "20–24 meters," or "more than 200 hectares"). And make logical connections between sentences. Don't assume that the reader can fill in all the missing ideas. If you say, for example, that logs are chipped to save labor, this may not make sense unless you have provided appropriate background. It might seem, to the reader, that the most labor-saving approach would be to leave the logs alone and to not chip them at all!

Avoid pretentious or verbose terminology Mark Twain said that writers should strike out every third word on principle. Some variation of this practice can be helpful to you. When you have a choice between two words or phrases, use the simplest, the most straightforward and familiar. Call a spade a spade. Don't call it an "environmental manipulator."

Instead of:	Use:
At this point in time	Now
Utilize	Use
Demonstrate	Show
Has been shown to be	Is
In view of the fact that	Because
Accomplished	Done
In the majority of cases	Usually
Despite the fact that	Although
Implement	Carry out
Viable	Practical (or workable)
Approximately	About

Delete phrases such as "It was found that . . .," "It should perhaps be noted here that . . . ," or "It is generally accepted that. . . ."

Consider the following passage:[30]

> In order to evaluate the possible significance of certain molecular parameters at the subcellular level, and to shed light on the conceivable role of structural configuration in spatial relationships of intracellular macromolecules, an integrated approach to the problem of cell diffusivity has been devised and developed. The results, which are in a preliminary stage, are discussed here in some detail because of their possible implication in mechanisms of diffusivity in a wider sphere.

Without verbosity, pomposity, fashionable circumlocutions, dangling constructions, and polysyllables, the same passage might look like this:

> To determine the molecular size and shape of A and B, I measured their sedimentation and diffusion constants. Results are given in

Table 1. They show that A is a roughly spherical molecule of molecular weight 36,000. The molecular weight of B remains uncertain since the sample seems to be impure. This is being further investigated.

Avoid overspecialized language Limit use of jargon. Whenever you can, use words that are familiar to a lot of people. It is tempting to make excuses for fogging up your writing with long sentences and big words ("My topic is very complex . . ."), but you are writing for a broader audience than you might at first think. You are writing for all those who might want or need to know about some aspect of your work, not just for the dozen or so who are doing exactly your kind of work. If special terminology is readily understandable to this broader audience, use it. If not, use more standardized terminology or carefully define the terms you are using. Define terms such as anisotropic, broadcast burning, canker, air quality, root collar, smolts, and tool life. You might use a parenthetical statement or a full-sentence definition following the first use of the word. In general, don't present any new idea or word without giving information to clarify it.

Use the active voice Avoid all forms of the verb "to be"—is, was, are, were, and so on. For example, "Nutrients are moved to the crown by the sapstream" becomes "The sapstream moves nutrients to the crown." "Shown in Figure 6 is . . ." becomes "Figure 6 shows. . . ."

For various reasons, students making their first attempts at technical writing believe it impolite or otherwise inappropriate to

Why didn't he just say: "All the fish died!"

FIGURE 7-1 *(Source: Thompson, E.T.,* How to Write Clearly, *reprinted with permission from International Paper Company, 1982.)*

use first-person pronouns. Instead of a concise and straightforward "I compared . . . ," we get "A comparison was made between. . . ." Worse is reference to "the author" or "the present writer," as if avoidance of a personal pronoun can divert any blame for the work to some ghostlike entity other than the student. Such usage is pretentious, verbose, and imprecise.

Be positive   Avoid an apologetic tone, especially in recounting your results. In the numerous instances where you describe something that didn't go as planned, write it in a straightforward, unapologetic manner. Say what you did and what you found, not what you didn't do or find. If you had planned to sample 10 trees in each stand, but were able to sample only 3 in some of them, don't apologize. You can say, for example, "Because of the low level of bark beetle infestation in several stands, the number of trees sampled over the 25 stands varied from 3 to 10 (Table 4)."

Use verb tenses appropriately   Pay attention to past, present, and future tenses. Use these tenses to distinguish clearly (both in your own mind and for the readers) between facts and generalizations. When recounting *factual* information from published literature (in the introduction), or from your own work (in methods and results), use the past tense. For example, "Average length of fish caught from 1975 to 1979 decreased by 25% (Smith 1980)." When you recount any *generalization,* from the past literature or from your own work, use the present tense. For example, "Overuse of reservoirs for recreational fishing harms the fish population." Other indicators of generalizations—especially ones about which you aren't terribly confident—are words such as "may," "suggest," and "could."

WRITING THE THESIS

Approach
Steps in writing are (1) organization, (2) writing the first draft, and (3) revising. Most people begin organizing their material with an outline. The outline, like a map, tells how you will arrive at your destination, the completed thesis. If you have a work plan,

however rudimentary it may be, this can form part of your thesis outline. The parts of a thesis outlined below will give you an idea of how to structure the information you have gathered. If you are using a different format—a journal style, for example—use that to develop your outline.

As you outline your work and reconstruct the events and discoveries of the past few years, think of yourself as a storyteller. There are many important and obvious similarities between a thesis and a story. Both are written to tell others something. They are written for readers. They both have a beginning, a middle, and an end. Words, ideas, and facts that are included in them are all relevant to the story in some way. As you work up your outline, you will probably find that some of the literature review that you accumulated earlier in developing your work plan may not be relevant to the story you are now trying to tell, and that additional information may be needed. Consider the relation of all your accumulated information to the topic at hand and exclude extraneous details. For example, a brief account of the life history of a species may be pertinent, but an anatomical description may not, and vice versa. If you are terribly fond of a section you worked hard on earlier but that has little direct relevance to the story, put it aside and later try to convince your advisor that it should at least be included in an appendix.

Because you are writing for several different types of readers, the basic idea is to maintain a simple story line and to include all the necessary detail in such a way that it is there for those who wish to read it, but it doesn't get in the way of those who don't or can't. This goal is achieved by using different levels of detail in different sections of the thesis. The introduction and the discussion should be interesting and easily understandable to any scientifically literate reader. If parts of the introduction get too obscure, put them in the literature review or an appendix. The introduction and the discussion alone should tell your story effectively to 90 percent of the people who might want to read your thesis. Methods and results can be fairly detailed and complex, since they will be read primarily by those in the specific research area or closely related areas. Just as you must assume different mental attitudes to generate ideas or carry out experiments, you must switch styles of writing in your thesis so that it becomes readable and understandable to the maximum number of potential readers.

It may also help to think of the completed thesis as being first deductive (going from the general to the specific) and then inductive (going from the specific to the general) (Figure 7-2). Start the introduction with some general background. Out of this background develop the problem and questions that you will address. From this problem area, delineate a set of very specific objectives. Your methods and results are extremely specific. They relate directly back to your objectives. In your results section, begin to make summaries of your findings, and start going back to generalities. In your discussion, interpret your findings, going from specific results to generalizations about the value of the work and its relationship to the overall problem area defined in the introduction. This style of writing provides continuity and makes it easier for you to write and the reader to read.

The First Draft

Writing the first draft, or at least major sections of the first draft, should be done in a few long sittings. Once you begin writing, continue writing. If you can't think of the right word or have temporarily forgotten the source of a reference, insert a blank or a question mark. If you need a fact you don't have on hand, do the same. The point is to not interrupt your flow of thought. Keep going until you come to a logical stopping place, then go a little beyond. Start the next section. This will make it easier to get started again later. Leaving the next section unfinished will activate your subconscious to start working on it, and the transition between sections will read more smoothly.

Writing your first draft rapidly is necessary because writing, like walking, is a dynamic process. One foot is up, your weight shifts, and you can't stay still. You start and the rest follows. You have to take another step and another. Once you have your outline and an assortment of facts ready to go, one written word will bring another, so go as fast as you can, even though you may not feel that what you are writing is very coherent. The creative process will be squelched if you stop to critically evaluate your work or to add details at this stage.

THE THESIS

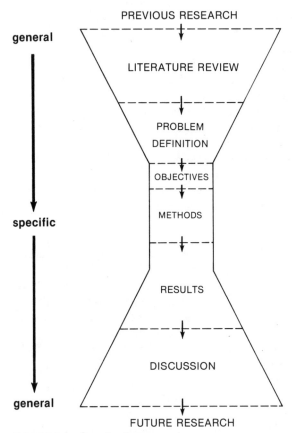

FIGURE 7-2 The "flow" of research.

Once you've written a crude first draft, go over it to fill in details and smooth out the wording. If you have difficulty with a section, try telling someone what you are trying to say. The words may come. Shift things around to get them in the best order. If you aren't using a word processor, use scissors and tape to reassemble entire sections.

After you have edited and revised your first draft, give it to someone else, such as your advisor, for comments and criticism. Because most faculty members realize how difficult it is to get going on the complete thesis, your advisor will probably be happy to see your initial efforts even though, at this point, the draft itself will be far from satisfying your (or your advisor's) concept of what the final thesis should be.

Solicit advice from other people—from anyone whose opinion you respect. If someone's suggestions are helpful, say "Thank you" and use them. If you disagree with them, say "Thank you" and don't use them. It is your work and you must make the decisions. However, with your advisor and committee members, be sure to work out conflicting points of view in an amiable and earnest way before the final thesis defense. The final exam is no place to enter with unresolved differences of opinion between you and your committee. (This same advice holds true for a Ph.D. preliminary examination that focuses on a student's research proposal.)

Expect your thesis to go through at least three to four complete revisions before it can go to your committee. It is often best to submit a section at a time to your advisor for review, at least during writing of the very first draft. After a complete draft goes to your committee, you will probably have to revise it at least twice more. Expect your advisor and other members of your committee to take 1 to 2 weeks to review each draft. If time is short, some people can be prodded to do this more quickly. Others may have to be reminded of your need for the review several times before you get it back, even after a week or two.

You will increase the quality and effectiveness of your writing if you let time elapse between drafts. Each time you come back to it, you will see it with new eyes. Good writers consider editing and review integral parts of the writing process, not just a final polishing. Any good writing was rewritten and revised several times before it reached its final form. Writing your thesis will teach you the necessity for repeated review and revision of your work.

Thesis guides more than a year or two old give advice on finding and working with a typist as you write your thesis. The increasingly widespread availability of word processors now means that most students can type and edit their own theses, often through the final draft. By all means learn to use any word-processing facility that may be available. If you must use a typist, be sure to find one who has a word processor with letter-quality printing capabilities for the final draft.

Because writing clarifies thought, thesis writing will reveal gaps in your work that you hadn't noticed before. For this reason, you will not be twiddling your thumbs while your advisor or committee is reviewing a draft of your thesis. After a flurry of writing activity on each draft, you will find yourself running back to the library, computer terminal, laboratory, or field to gather last-minute bits of information to flesh out your thesis, making it more complete. Most former graduate students will tell you that they learned more during the last few months of their program than they did in all the preceding years of undergraduate and graduate study. Many say that their most fruitful experiments or observations were made between thesis drafts.

There is no clear distinction between doing research and writing about it. The two activities complement and stimulate each other. So don't ever think that you should somehow feel that your research is finished before you begin writing your thesis in earnest. Start writing long before the last test is run.

PARTS OF A THESIS

As you approach writing the thesis to meet a university or self-imposed deadline, obtain and read carefully whatever specifications there may be for the report—paper, type style, binding, illustrations, and other matters of format and presentation. If you don't understand these, ask for clarification. Understanding and following these specifications from the beginning will save you time in the end.

Title page and abstract The format for a title page is standard for most institutions. Check your graduate handbook or previous theses. The abstract is generally the same as the abstract in a proposal (see page 75), except that it contains a summary of results and is sometimes two or three pages long. For Ph.D. theses going onto microfilm, abstracts are limited to 350 words (which is still two to three pages). Although it is often written last, the abstract is usually the first part of your report to be read. If it is not interesting, it will be the *only* part read.

Vitae   Sometimes a vitae is also listed as a part of the thesis. If at all possible, don't include one. If you are moving ahead with your life and career, your vitae will be out of date within months.

Acknowledgments   Acknowledgments are an important part of the thesis. Their central elements are simple courtesy and professionalism. They should be direct and sincere. If you have kept detailed records of your research and cooperators, writing your acknowledgments will not be difficult. Traditionally, one starts by thanking the major advisor and the committee and then moves on to others, telling what role each played in the work. Avoid stilted or pompous language. "I thank . . ." is preferable to "I want to take this opportunity to express my gratitude to . . .," "Deep gratitude is extended to . . .," or "I wish to acknowledge my gratitude to. . . ." Acknowledge any outside financial assistance, such as grants, contracts, or fellowships: "This research was supported by a grant from. . . ." A long acknowledgments section is a good sign that the student has started to build a solid network of professional contacts.

Table of contents   The table of contents and lists of tables and figures should be self-explanatory. Use a lot of headings and subheadings throughout the thesis, and put these in the table of contents. Some advisors or departments prefer that tables and figures be integrated with the text—that is, appearing near where they are first mentioned in the body of the thesis. Only very long tables are put in the back of the thesis in an appendix. Other advisors or departments prefer a format similar to that submitted to a journal, with tables and figures grouped in the back of the thesis, between the list of references and any appendices.

Terminology and symbols   Theses and journal articles in some areas (such as engineering or mathematics) often start with a nomenclature section or a list of symbols. In some other research areas, a glossary is used when the topic crosses a number of disciplines. In most theses, simple definitions when new words first appear in the text are usually sufficient.

Introduction   Problem statement, objectives, and literature review may be handled separately or in a single introduction. Much of your introduction can be taken directly from your proposal and edited and expanded as necessary. The introduction should, above all, be readable and to a rather wide group of people. Introduce the reader gently and formally to the subject. Have a separate literature review if your introduction seems too long and potentially boring, but make sure that your introduction can stand alone, that it includes all your main points. Include in the literature review only details and elaboration of main points previously summarized in the introduction or problem statement. Feel free to use reference citations throughout the rest of the thesis—in the introduction, methods, results, and discussion—as needed. There is no rule that says reference citations belong only in the literature review.

Methods   The methods section should include a detailed, orderly account of what you did, reconstructed for brevity and clarity. Hindsight is important here. Koller[16] explained:

> The doers, the ones who do something really well, are taught a method. The method serves them, up to a point. But then some sureness about what they're trying to do lets them cast off that method, or start to. Something they know impels them to bridge the chasm that lies between the safe inadequacy of what they've been taught and the fulfillment that they uncertainly sense will exist on the other side. And the only way to get to what can't really be guaranteed but can only be hoped for is to make a leap. Once on the other side, they look back and then throw down a footbridge, their method, for their followers to use.

Methods should be clear enough that someone else could follow your account and repeat the work. Whenever possible, summarize your methods in tables or figures. If you are attempting to integrate tables and figures into the text, put excessively long tables and information not essential for general understanding of the methods in an appendix.

Results   Results are simply what you found—the facts—without interpretation. For this reason, the results and methods are usually the easiest parts of the thesis to write. Just as methods follow step by step from your objectives, results follow step by step from your methods. As with methods, you can include a fair amount of detail, since results are usually read only by people who are really involved or interested in doing such work themselves. However, use tables or figures whenever possible and, in the text, only summarize the key findings presented in the tables.

Discussion   Your discussion tells what the work means, how your results can be interpreted in light of your stated objectives. You are not obligated to interpret every result obtained. Present only the "goodies" in the discussion. Do not recapitulate your results. The discussion presents principles, relationships, and generalizations arising from your work. Point out any exceptions or any lack of correlations, and define unsettled points. Show how your results and interpretations agree (or contrast) with previously published work. Discuss theoretical and practical implications of your work.

Conclusions   Requirements for conclusions, a summary, or recommendations depend upon the research area and the individual institution's or advisor's preferences. An abstract and a summary are much alike, so you rarely find both in the same paper. Each reviews the main points of the paper from beginning to end. They must be complete in themselves. They should start with a problem statement or hypothesis and end with its evaluation.

Conclusions reiterate only your main findings (results and generalizations). If recommendations are presented as a separate section, they include new information and suggestions for applications of the work and for future research that were not presented earlier. If these sections are not required or considered appropriate as separate sections, you must still build a summary of your findings into the abstract and put recommendations for future work in your discussion.

Literature cited Follow your institution's required format for literature cited. Most commonly, references are presented in an alphabetized list. In the text, citations can be given as either the author's name and the year of publication, or numbers in parentheses. (Number references in the literature-cited section only if the second format is used.) For articles with only one or two authors, both names are usually given—for example, Smith (1970) or Smith and Johnson (1982). If the paper has three or more authors, the citation is often shortened to, for example, Smith et al. (1981).

Appendices A thesis is often considered a repository for all information pertinent to the research project. In your appendices, you can put your raw data, recipes for solutions or stains, questionnaires, maps, computer programs, calibration curves, circuit diagrams, and any other details of methods and results that would clutter the body of the thesis unnecessarily.

JOURNAL ARTICLES

The primary aim of a journal article is to present something new and to show its validity by describing in some detail the testing process used to validate it. The process of proof is emphasized and the processes whereby the ideas were generated and refined is often condensed drastically. Imaginative processes and modifications of the original problem statement and hypotheses are usually omitted. Only the final version of the problem statement or hypothesis is presented, along with the evidence supporting or refuting it. Alternative approaches that did not work out are usually omitted. Only a rather general statement of objectives is usually given. As in a thesis, the test part of the research process is described in detail in the methods and results section. In terms of adding to our knowledge, the really important part of the article is, as in the thesis, the discussion, where the meaning of the work is presented and generalizations are made.

Even if it is not required at your institution, consider transforming your thesis into an article for publication as the next logical step in the communication process. The publication process can be facilitated by preparing the thesis with a particular journal in mind and, where the journal's format does not conflict with that required for the thesis, using the journal's style in writing the thesis.

Authorship

Authorship of a publication is usually a simple issue. The person who does most of the research writes the paper and automatically becomes its sole or senior (first-listed) author. However, authorship sometimes becomes more complicated. As you have seen, there are a lot of things involved in producing a graduate research thesis, and many additional steps are necessary before the thesis becomes a journal article. Some of these steps are:

> Having the idea or deciding on the topic of investigation
> Financing the project or providing the facilities for doing it
> Planning the work and designing the experiments
> Doing the tests
> Interpreting results
> Writing the thesis
> Writing the paper for publication

Some researchers believe that the senior author is the person who did the majority of the work or the one who provided the funding. Others believe that senior authorship goes to the person who had the idea in the first place. Perhaps the most common rule of thumb is that the senior author is the person who designed the project, and the junior (second-listed) author is the one who did the work or wrote the paper. However, because of the effort involved in writing the paper for publication, some believe that senior authorship goes to the writer, regardless of who did the work and who wrote the thesis.

Changing a thesis into a paper for publication usually involves condensing it, having figures redrawn professionally, and writing it in a manner appropriate for a particular journal, as well as having it reviewed, revising it again, submitting it to the journal, handling review comments, and coming up with any page or reprint charges. However, to expedite the publication process, many research advisors are very willing to provide a great deal of help and still be only junior author.

Authorship does not generally go to people who were only involved in collecting data or doing the analyses ("number crunching"). These tasks could be done by any qualified technician and don't, by themselves, require any understanding of the research process as a whole. If data of others are used, an acknowledgment is warranted. However, although number crunching itself does not justify authorship, participation in selection of the experimental design or analytical technique to solve the problem is worthy of consideration for authorship. Interpretation of data is also an important part of the research process, and someone who helps substantially with this might also be considered for coauthorship.

Assuming that your major advisor has had a significant role in the development of your research project, and has supported it with advice during your graduate program, it is usually expected that, when you write up your thesis for publication, he or she will be junior author or at least should be offered junior authorship. This is not only a matter of common courtesy, but serves other purposes as well. As a relative unknown in research circles, having your name linked to someone who is better known can be helpful professionally. Also, having your advisor as a coauthor sometimes means that he or she will find the funds for publication and buying reprints, not a minor consideration when page charges for some journals range up to $100 per page and a single article plus reprints can run over $500.

STEPS TOWARD PUBLICATION

The first decision you need to make when you decide to publish your thesis is which journal you should submit it to. It is helpful to make this choice when you begin writing the thesis, as your choice will affect your writing style. Two general criteria pertain. First, choose a journal that deals with your general subject area—for example, one that you have cited frequently in your literature review. Second, pick a good journal, a fairly prestigious one. Just because it is your first paper, don't think that you should put it in some little-known journal with limited distribution. Select a journal that is widely read (perhaps one that goes with membership in your main professional society) and in which articles are refereed (critically reviewed) before they are accepted. Nonrefereed journals do not count, professionally, as much as articles in refereed journals.

Unfortunately, the best journals are sometimes expensive, but don't make finances the main criterion for choice of a journal. Even expensive journals sometimes waive or at least reduce costs for people paying out of their own pockets, and funding can often be obtained through your department chairperson or major advisor, especially if he or she is one of the authors. Discuss the issue of cost with your advisor, even if you have already left school and are working elsewhere.

Instructions to Authors

Once you have selected a journal, look in recent issues for "instructions to authors" or "information for contributors." These are often found inside the front or back cover of the journal. In some journals they are less easy to find, but realize that such instructions exist somewhere in issues of the past year. (Some journals just refer to a particular style manual, such as the *Council of Biology Editors Style Manual.*) These instructions give you essential details for publishing in that particular journal. Follow them to the letter for format (for example, how to handle headings and subheadings, how to cite references), treatment of tables and figures, number of copies to submit, where to send them, and so on. If details of format are not provided or are not clear, look at recent articles in that journal to see how they are done.

In general, a manuscript for publication includes a title page, giving title, authors, and their addresses. The name and address of the corresponding author is repeated in the upper right-hand corner, and the name of the journal to which the article is being submitted is listed in the upper left. List as your address the institution where the work was done, even if you are currently working elsewhere. As a footnote, add your "Present address. . . ." This ensures that the institution gets full credit for the research, as is appropriate. The text of the article usually includes an abstract, introduction, methods, results, discussion, acknowledgments, and references. These are followed by tables, figure captions (on a single page), and figures (with no captions), in that order.

You are asked to submit, along with the appropriate number of copies of the full manuscript (including copies of figures), originals of figures. If you have no training in graphic arts, and no ready access to quality advice in these matters, pay to have your figures done professionally. Nothing makes a paper look more amateurish than poor illustrations. In the upper corner or back of each figure, list (in blue pencil) authors, address, abbreviated title, and figure number. "Originals" can be, and usually is, interpreted to mean high-quality copies—photographs of some type—while you keep the actual originals or replicates of the originals in your office for safekeeping. As always, you should never send off your only good copy. It is safest to assume that any part of what you send to anyone can be misplaced, so keep a backup copy of the most recent version of your manuscript at each stage, as well as originals of figures. The figures that are attached to each review copy of your manuscript can simply be photocopies.

As a carry-over from the olden days of carbon copies, some journals request, for example, "two copies plus the original." Because modern photocopies turn out as clear as, and often clearer than, the original, it is perfectly acceptable to submit three good photocopies and to retain the original in your own files. This is a fortunate development because it means you can really work over the original—cutting and taping to rearrange sections, whiting out words, or typing over entire lines that have been covered with white correcting tape. All such manuscript surgery, if done carefully, is undetectable in a good photocopy. Using a word processor, of course, would save you much of this effort.

Camera-Ready Copy

To speed up the publication process, many meeting proceedings and even some journals are now asking for final reviewed drafts of manuscripts in camera-ready form. Camera-ready copy refers to manuscript pages that are ready to be photocopied and presented as is, usually in typewriter-like printing. The author is thus almost totally responsible for the final content and appearance of his or her published paper. The final product doesn't look quite as professional and "finished" as a typeset article, but the speed of publication may be much greater and costs considerably lower.

Sequence of Events

First, revise your thesis, cutting it up and making it more concise and to the point, using the appropriate journal format. The thesis rewrite should be much shorter than the thesis, with highly selected tables and figures. The time lapse between completion of the thesis and working on the publication gives you a fresh perspective that facilitates this condensation and rewriting process. When you and your other author(s) agree that it is at least acceptable, if not ideal, subject it to your own review process. Give copies to two or more people in your specialty area who can criticize the paper and help improve it further. Accompany these manuscripts (even those given to a person in the same building) with a letter or note asking for candid comments, saying which journal you plan to submit it to (even though this information also appears on the paper's title page), and saying when you would like to have comments back. (Three weeks is about the minimum.) If you don't have the review copies back by about your stated time plus a week or two, it is appropriate to write or call the reviewers and politely ask how they are doing as you are looking forward to incorporating their suggestions in your revision of the article. In some cases, you will just have to give up; some manuscripts go out and are never seen again because a particular reviewer might be bogged down with work at that time or because he or she cannot or will not review it for other reasons. That is why it is important to send copies to several people. It is not necessary to know a reviewer personally. Often asking someone to review a manuscript is a good way to initiate a long-term professional relationship.

Don't be too disappointed if some of the manuscripts come back with very few helpful comments on them. A rigorous review is the exception rather than the rule, and you must look long and hard, over many years, to find even two or three people who will really help you out consistently with their comments. Accept all reviews, especially the most detailed and critical, with good grace. Thank-you letters are appropriate. Include reviewers' names in your acknowledgments section, and, when the paper finally appears in print, send each reviewer a signed reprint with repeated thanks.

Once you get the reviews back (realistically, allow up to 2 months unless you are seriously pressured by deadlines), revise your paper, tidy it up again, and submit it to the journal. Include in a large envelope (don't fold anything) the appropriate number of copies of the complete manuscript (with tables and figures on each), your "original" figures, and a cover letter saying something like, "Enclosed are———copies of a manuscript entitled '———' by ——— and ———. We would like this paper to be considered for publication in [name of journal]."

It is understood that you are not submitting the manuscript to more than one journal. You may submit the article to another journal only if it is rejected or you withdraw it from the first journal's review process. If some of the information has appeared in preliminary or general form in a nonrefereed publication, you can still submit it to a journal, but you can't repeat the same research article in two places.

When the journal receives the manuscript, you may receive a postcard or note acknowledging its receipt. Then the editor will send the article out to two or three of the journal's reviewers. At this point, who reviews your paper is pretty much up to fate, though you can suggest appropriate reviewers to the editor. A word of warning is needed, however. The people who know you and your work best often make a very strong effort to be objective when the journal sends them one of your papers for review. These people sometimes give much more rigorous and critical reviews than people who don't know you. Not worrying about who will review your paper is generally the best policy.

Your overall sense of objectivity is sometimes shaken by the range of variation in journal reviews, though, in general, the reviewers will come up with the same ballpark estimate of your manuscript's merit. Each journal reviewer usually gets the chance to choose between verdicts of accept as is, accept with minor revision, accept with major revision, or reject. Based on the consensus of all reviewers, the editor sends the decision to you, along with unsigned copies of the reviewers' comments. So even if your paper is rejected, you will usually have detailed critiques to help you identify the problem.

Rejection is often a crushing blow when it is your first attempt at publication, but it happens to all of us, especially in the beginning, and becomes much less painful and, fortunately, less common with time. Not taking such rejection personally is easy when you have several publications under your belt, but if it is your first, you probably will take it personally. Put the article aside after reading the reviews. Take time to assimilate the information and to regain your good spirits. When you recover, get back to your manuscript as soon as possible. Having your first paper accepted as is, or even with minor revisions, is something akin to a miracle, so don't expect it. Set your hopes on an "accept with major revision" and you probably won't be disappointed. In my experience at least, papers are rarely accepted with no changes needed.

It may be consoling to realize that there is not always a very direct relationship between the quality of the work in a scientific sense, and its rating by the reviewers. According to Swindel and Perry's[29] Golden Rule of the Arts and Sciences, the probability of a manuscript being accepted by referees is related to the quality of the manuscript by the Gaussian (normal) curve (Figure 7-3). Trivial and very traditional sorts of research are often easier to get published than are more interesting ones, especially if a nonstandard approach was used. In general the more innovative the work and the more it contradicts accepted beliefs and assumptions, the

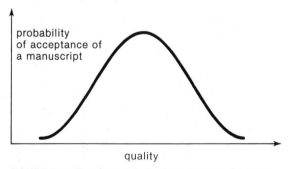

FIGURE 7-3   The Golden Rule of the Arts and Sciences.

more trouble you will have getting it accepted. The best sort of research results make people rethink and revise their understanding, and only the most open-minded people find that nonthreatening, especially from a newcomer. Reviewers will often suggest that you tone down your enthusiasm a bit, that you limit the generalizations you are making about the work. If you can't do this, or just plain don't want to do what the reviewers recommend, you always have the option to withdraw the paper (politely with a letter to the editor) and send it somewhere else.

Assuming, however, that you are able to take the criticism in a constructive manner (and even caustic reviews usually contain useful comments), you need to read the reviews carefully and incorporate the necessary revisions and changes into your manuscript. A safe and expedient tactic—though not necessarily a progressive one—is to cut out items that reviewers don't like, rather than going to great lengths to make them acceptable. It is painful to feel that you are gutting the paper by doing this, but journals and reviewers are a generally conservative lot, and what you may cherish as some of your cleverest ideas and insights may, for the time being, have to fall by the wayside.

Revise the manuscript as best you can. You don't have to address every criticism by the reviewers. Send the revised manuscript back to the editor with a letter saying that you have incorporated the suggestions of the reviewers. You don't need to detail your response to all the reviewers' comments, but it's a good idea to point out any major changes that you made and to explain why you didn't change something that seems an important issue to a reviewer. If there are some things that you didn't change, and feel that you have a good reason not to, say so simply and positively. For example, "We decided to retain the terminology for ——— as originally submitted as this is consistent with the major review papers in this particular area."

If all goes well, the next step is a note or card from the editor saying that your manuscript has been accepted for publication. Some time later—often several months later—you will receive, by mail, galley proofs and, sometimes, a bill. Galley proofs are the first rough typesetting of your paper. They look much like the final published article but give you the chance for a final proofreading.

Do this promptly and carefully. You will nearly always find at least a few minor typographical errors and occasionally very large errors or omissions. Carefully proofread figure legends, tables, and reference citations; these areas often have the most errors. Use a red pencil and mark changes and corrections clearly in the margins. If at all possible, galleys should be sent back to the journal within 48 hours. Any page changes or reprint costs are to be paid at this time. It is not necessary to send the purchase order or check with the galleys, but include a note saying that a purchase order will follow (and make sure that it does).

Because of the long time delay between doing the work and writing about it, your ideas and research findings will probably have advanced by the time you receive reviews or galleys from the journal. You can add qualifying statements to the final revision (alluding to ongoing work, perhaps) and even change the galleys, though this may cost you additional typesetting fees. But if you realize that by the time your paper comes out it will probably be out-of-date as far as you're concerned, this disparity between your present research and the paper that is being published will not concern you unduly. The article represents a time in the past—an earlier state of your work. You will go completely crazy if you attempt to update the information contained in the paper each time it returns to you during the publication process.

Finally, at some unspecified later time, the article will appear in print. If you don't subscribe to the journal and don't regularly check the library for new issues, your first indication that your paper is out is often a reprint request from some enthusiastic and earnest soul. However, reprints themselves will often arrive weeks or even months after the paper is published, so, for the time being, just stockpile reprint requests.

Until you actually send your manuscript to the journal, the paper can only be considered "in preparation." (Don't, however, list a paper as "in preparation" when it exists only as a clever idea in your head!) Between the time you mail the paper and the time it is either rejected or accepted, it is "submitted for publication." Once it is accepted, you may call the paper "in press." The paper becomes an official publication once you have the year, volume, and page numbers. Some journals or styles require that you refer to any work as "unpublished" or cite it in a footnote until it actually appears in print, though the categories mentioned above can be used in a résumé or vitae.

WRITING A REVIEW

At some time in your research career, either during graduate school or later on, you will begin to have opportunities to review (or critique) the work of others. Your advisor might pass along review requests or, through contacts made at professional meetings or in the course of your work, other researchers in your area will ask for your comments on research proposals or manuscripts being prepared for publication. Eventually you will begin to get manuscripts from the journals themselves. Writing reviews is a lot of work, but it is an important part of the job of a researcher. Reviewing is a favor you exchange with your colleagues, and it permits you to obtain up-to-date information on research in your area. All review requests should be handled conscientiously even if, in a crisis, you can only return the manuscript promptly saying that you cannot review it at the time.

Here are some suggestions on how to approach doing a review. First, read the article over carefully, making notes (in pencil if you make them on the manuscript itself) of both a specific and general nature. As in oral presentations, keep in mind the two aspects of the paper that you will critique: content (the subject matter or ideas expressed) and style (their manner of presentation). As you read the paper, note any aspects of either content or style that strike you as particularly good or particularly bad. If a point is obscure, a definition or clarification needed, note these also. It can help to outline the paper with a V (see Chapter 3). This technique quickly identifies both the strong and weak points of a research paper. Use all your knowledge of the research process, writing, and communicating in general. The principles you have learned about these subjects apply directly to reviewing the work of others.

For content, ask yourself questions such as: Was sufficient background information given so that I could understand why the research was done? Were definitions provided where appropriate?

Were the objectives clear? Was the significance of the work clear? Did the work seem relevant and useful, or at least interesting? For style, ask yourself: Is the paper well written? Clear? Concise? Is the meaning of tables and figures clear? Are figures of professional quality?

Type the review on a separate piece of paper, even if you have annotated the manuscript extensively . If you are reviewing for a journal, a review sheet is usually provided. In reviews to individuals, you may want to write the review as the body of a letter. In any case, whenever possible, start the review with a statement of a general and positive nature (such as, "This is a well-written paper about a very new and interesting research area."). Say something nice, but true, about the overall paper. Next, make some specific and detailed statements about the good points of the paper. When this is done, point out the weak points and suggest how they might be improved or revised. Good reviews are never harsh, personal, sarcastic, or belittling. Give constructive criticisms, adding useful suggestions as to how the person might have made your review more positive. Don't hesitate to say how you would have liked to have seen the paper written. Most of your notes within the manuscript itself should be self-explanatory, but you might want to itemize comments, page by page, in your review as well. Return both the review and the manuscript to the author or journal. Until the proposed research is presented publicly, or the paper appears in published form, your knowledge of its contents should be considered confidential.

REFERENCES

1   Bernard, C., *An Introduction to the Study of Experimental Medicine,* Macmillan, New York, 1865 (English translation 1927).

2   Beveridge, W. I. B., *The Art of Scientific Investigation,* W. W. Norton, New York, 1961.

3   Bragg, L., Talking About Science, *Science,* **154:**1613–1616 (1966).

4   Campbell, J. P., R. L. Daft, and C. L. Hulin, *What to Study: Generating and Developing Research Questions,* Sage Publications, Beverly Hills, Calif., 1982.

5   Clance, P., and J. Imes, The Impostor Phenomenon in High Achieving Women: Dynamics and Therapeutic Interaction, *Psychotherapy: Theory, Research and Practice,* **15:**241–247 (1978).

6   Davis, M. S., That's Interesting! Toward a Phenomenology of Sociology and a Sociology of Phenomenology, *Philosophy of Social Science,* 1:309–344, 1971.

7   Davis, R. M., *Thesis Projects in Science and Engineering,* St. Martin's, New York, 1980.

8   Day, R. A., *How to Write and Publish a Scientific Paper,* ISI Press, Philadelphia, 1979.

9   Dewey, J., *How We Think,* D. C. Heath, Boston, 1933.

10 Dunkle, T., Obfuscatory Scrivenery (Foggy Writing), *Science 82,* **3**(3):82–84 (1982).

11 Eaves, G. N., Who Reads Your Project-Grant Application to the National Institutes of Health? *Federation Proceedings,* **31**(1):2–9 (1972).

12 Eisenberg, A., *Effective Technical Communication,* McGraw-Hill, New York, 1982.

13 Gowin, D. B., *Educating,* Cornell Univ. Press, Ithaca, N.Y., 1981.

14 Kendig, F., A Conversation with Roger Schank, *Psychology Today,* **17**(4):28–34 (1983).

15 Kerlinger, F. N., *Foundations of Behavioral Research: Education and Psychological Inquiry,* 2d ed., Holt, Rinehart and Winston, New York, 1964.

16 Koller, A., *An Unknown Woman: A Journey to Self-Discovery,* Bantam, New York, 1981.

17 Kuhn, T. S., *The Structure of Scientific Revolutions,* 2d ed., Univ. of Chicago Press, 1970.

18 Lightman, A., Nothing But the Truth, *Science 82,* **4**(4):24–26 (1982).

19 Maltz, M., *Psycho-cybernetics,* Prentice-Hall, Englewood Cliffs, New Jersey, 1960.

20 McGregor, D., *The Human Side of Enterprise,* McGraw-Hill, New York, 1960.

21 Medawar, P. B., *Advice to a Young Scientist,* Harper & Row, New York, 1979.

22 Nord, M. A., The Design and Delivery of Effective Oral Presentations, *Proc. National Meeting of the Society of Women Engineers,* Seattle, June 1983, pp. 120–122.

23 Rubin, Z., The Bright Side of Poverty, *Psychology Today,* **15**(10):8–13 (1981).

24 Russell, B., *The Conquest of Happiness,* Liveright, New York, 1930.

25 Sindermann, C. L., *Winning the Games Scientists Play,* Plenum, New York, 1982.

26 Stammel, M., 50 Ways to Leave Your Mentor, *Savvy,* **4**(9):20–22 (1983).

27 Sternberg, D., *How to Complete and Survive a Doctoral Dissertation,* St. Martin's, New York, 1981.

28 Strunk, W., and E. B. White, *The Elements of Style,* 2d ed., Macmillan, New York, 1972.

Look at time manage. Books
How to put more time in your life.
Orn Scott PhD

29 Swindel, B. F., and T. O. Perry, A Previously Unannounced Form of the Gaussian Distribution: The Golden Rule of Arts and Sciences, *J. Irreprod. Results,* **21**(3):8–9 (1975).
30 Woodford, F. P., Sounder Thinking through Clearer Writing, *Science,* 156:743–745 (1967).

Index